MW00636068

PROFESSIONAL TENNIS DRILLS

by

Laszlo Leiter

MW00636068

PTD Publishing
© Copyright 2012

Library of Congress Data

Professional Tennis Drills
by Laszlo Leiter
Registration Number: TX 7-576-534
ISBN: 978-0-9852637-2-0

No guarantee is given that the information provided in this book is correct, complete, and/or up-to-date. The materials contained in this book are provided for general information purposes only and do not constitute legal or other professional advice on any subject matter. The author does not accept any responsibility for any loss which may arise from reliance on information contained in this book. The contents of this book are protected by copyright under international conventions and the reproduction or retransmission of the contents of this book is prohibited without the prior written consent of the author. This book and its contents are provided "AS IS" without warranty of any kind, either express or implied, including, but not limited to, the implied warranties of merchantability, fitness for a particular purpose, or non-infringement. Reproduction, distribution, republication, and/or retransmission of material contained within this book

are prohibited unless the prior written permission of PTD Publishing has been obtained.

This book is dedicated to my family

for their never ending support.

Contents

About the Creators...1

About the Book..2

Understanding the Drills Section...3

Private Lessons...5
    Warm-up..5
    Ground strokes 8
    Net approach 12
    Net play 15
    Serve and return 19

Semi-private Lessons **26**
    Warm-up..26
    Ground strokes 29
    Net approach 33
    Net play 36
    Serve and return 40
    Footwork 44

Three Player Lessons **48**
    Warm-up..48
    Ground strokes 52
    Net approach 55
    Net play 59
    Serve and return 63
    Footwork 67

Four Player Lessons **71**
    Warm-up..71
    Ground strokes 75
    Net approach 78
    Net play 82
    Serve and return 86
    Footwork 90

Clinics...**94**
    Warm-up..94
    Ground strokes 98
    Net approach 102
    Net play 106
    Serve and return 109
    Footwork 113

Fun Drills...**118**

Multi Court Drills **128**
    Warm-up..128
    Ground strokes 131
    Net approach 135

    Net play 139

    Serve and return 144

Definitions **149**

Drill Sheet **152**

Notes...**154**

About the Creators

PTD is a network of USPTA, USPTR certified, and nationally recognized tennis coaches who contribute regularly to this collection. Our contributors come from every continent from many different countries including the US, Germany, Spain, Russia, Hungary, UAE, Australia, South Africa, and more. PTD consists of high-school and college coaches, tennis professionals working with top national players, tennis camp counselors, and tennis directors of very successful tennis programs. We believe that sharing information such as tennis drills is mutually beneficial to our staff as well as our readers.

We also believe that the best way to learn is through games and exercises with objectives. Working towards goals ensures focus that leads to intensity which is crucial to learning. Although repetition of a single stroke has its place in player development, PTD tennis drills are not about one dimensional stroke production. We believe that tennis is a game and it should be played and practiced as such.

Our goal at PTD was to collect the largest number of co-operative and competitive tennis drills that are engaging and fun!

Thank you for purchasing our collection, we hope it proves to be a very valuable resource!

Laszlo Leiter
PTD Founder

About the Book

A few years ago, a couple of tennis professionals started searching the Internet for more tennis drills. Surprisingly, they barely found anything except a couple of elementary drills here and there. The lack of information about tennis drills was disappointing. It seemed like that tennis professionals either wanted to keep their precious drills for themselves or they were just too busy sharing them. That's when we decided to start PTD. We began writing down and cataloging all the drills that we could find. PTD continues collecting games and drills to this day. We talk to tennis coaches, attend seminars, read books, look for any source that could lead us to more drills. And not just any drills. We are only interested in drills that are game-like and fun. We are searching for games that are exciting instead of mundane or boring. We witnessed too many tennis clinics with players just standing around looking bored. Such lessons burn out players and coaches alike. We have always preferred live ball drills where players could work towards a goal or achieve something. We knew that expanding one's knowledge base will make better tennis coaches on the long run. By writing this book, PTD wanted to help other coaches and players to understand more about teaching and learning tennis. Since PTD will collect more and more drills in the future, the book will be updated periodically. Just like a tennis player seeking perfection, this collection is never finished.

Understanding the Drills Section

When we started writing this book, we weren't sure how we should group the drills so they are easy to browse through. There are so many aspects that you can rank drills. Is it for doubles or singles, for advanced players or just beginners, is it focusing on ground strokes or volleys, etc. We think the way we categorized the book is the best way to understand and sort through this large amount of material.

Anytime an instructor teaches a lesson or clinic, he always has a goal in mind. Tennis drills have to focus on parts of the game that players want to improve. Keeping this in mind, in this book we made the number one priority category the focus of the drill. Most drills don't just allow you to practice one type of shot, like forehands or backhands. The best drills incorporate certain tactics or strategies to practice. Even though this book contains drills that focus on one single aspect or shot, most of the exercises are live drills that allow point play and games. The breakdown of the first category is the following: **Warm-up, Ground strokes, Net approach, Net play, Serve and return,** and **Footwork**. Chapter 6 "**Fun Drills**" in the drill section is the only exception. The main focus here is not only to practice certain shots or strategies but simply to have fun. These drills are a great introduction for young kids and beginners to the game of tennis. Of course, it doesn't mean that the rest of the drills in this book are not fun. It simply means that the main goal is to play games without too much instruction.

The second level of categories is **Skill level**. Certain drills would be very hard, if not impossible, for beginners to practice. Also, advanced players couldn't find any challenge in some of the beginner drills. Sorting the drills according to skill level just made sense. Since most of the drills in this book are live drills or games, a greater number of drills are recommended for intermediate or advanced players. At the beginning stages, it is best for players to practice certain shots separately. There's not as much need for game like drills. Once a player can keep the ball in play reasonably well, practicing drills starts to make much more sense.

The next category in each drill is the **Setup**. It describes the position of each player in the drill as well as the instructor's. It is very important for everyone to understand the roles they will be playing. In most drills, the court or courts are divided into sides A and B. From the instructor's standpoint, side A simply means the close side and side B the far side. The instructor can have one of three roles in each drill. He participates (plays), feeds the balls, or observes the points. The instructor's given role is indicated in the setup category. When the instructor participates in a drill, he simply plays the points just like any other participating player. Feeding the ball means to put it in play. The observing instructor can give pointers or advices for players between points. The starting positions for players are clarified in the "Definitions" section at the end of the book. Some drills require setting up targets. The instructor can decide the size of the targets based on the skill level of the players.

The **Description** category explains what everyone in the drill is doing. We didn't include any strategic or technical advice for any drill simply because we thought that it was the instructor's job. Every pro has a personal teaching style and can implement it when using these drills. In this category, we only wanted to describe the mechanics of the drills. The reason why we sometimes used very elementary language was for two reasons: to avoid confusion and to make sure beginning teaching pros will understand the instructions. It's not there to insult anybody's intelligence.

We thought it was important to include a rough estimate of time **Length**. It is the average time range that the given drill takes to complete. It is not to say that the drill can not take longer or shorter amount of time. However, it will help the instructor estimate and plan his whole lesson.

Finally, every drill includes one or more **Variation** section. Some drills can be tweaked or changed completely to create an entirely different drill. Certain drills have only minor changes to them while others have major rule changes. Variants provide instructors more options to personalize each drill. Of course, coaches can add their own changes and variations to the drills. The possibilities are endless.

It is possible that the some of the same drills are included in different chapters. The reason for this is that the book wasn't meant to be read from start to finish. Different instructors may only read the private lesson section; others may only be interested in the clinics. Also, some of the drills may work for different formats. For example, many four player drills are also suitable for clinics. We didn't want any one of our readers missing out on drills they could potentially use.

So here it is, enjoy!

Private Lessons

This drill section includes one-on-one instructions with the tennis instructor. Since there is only one player, there are more "dead ball drills" in this chapter. The instructor actively participates in many of the drills. Even though it is rare, many of these exercises may not be recommended for beginning teachers. Instructors should decide on their own if they are capable of completing the drill after reading the material. All of these drills require one court. The use of targets is fairly common in this section. Private lessons are best to target specific areas of the player's game. It is the best format for individual learning.

I. <u>Warm-up</u>

1.

Name: Mini Tennis
Focus: Warm-up
Skill level: Beginner, intermediate, advanced
Setup: The instructor starts behind the service line on side A. The player starts behind the service line on side B.
Description: The instructor and the player try to keep the ball in one service box as long as they can. Hard shots are not allowed. The goal is to reach 15 shots in a row.
Length: 5 min
Variation: The instructor and the player can play out the point in the service box. The first player to reach 10 points is the winner.

2.

Name: Deep Shot Warm-Up
Focus: Warm-up
Skill level: Intermediate, advanced
Setup: The player and the instructor start at the opposite baselines.
Description: The player tries to hit every ball between the service line and the baseline. The instructor keeps the ball in play by hitting it back to the player. The drill ends when the player reaches 30 points.
Length: 5-6 min
Variation: For more advanced players the instructor can place a line of balls halfway between his service line and baseline. The player has to hit all balls behind this line.

3.

Name: Placement Warm-Up
Focus: Warm-up
Skill level: Intermediate, advanced
Setup: Instructor starts on the deuce side on side A. The player starts in the middle of his baseline on side B.
Description: The instructor hits every ball close to the player. The player can only hit to the deuce side of the court back to the instructor. The goal is to get to 10 shots in a row in. Then the instructor moves to the ad side and the drill is repeated.
Length: 10-12 min
Variation: The instructor can make it more challenging for the player by hitting balls further away from him.

4.

Name: Volley Warm-up
Focus: Warm-up
Skill level: Intermediate, advanced
Setup: Both the player and instructor start in front the T on the opposite sides.
Description: The player and instructor hit volleys back and forth. They try to keep the ball in the air without bouncing. The goal is to reach 20 volleys in a row.
Length: 5 min
Variation: The instructor and the player can volley from deuce side to deuce side and ad side to ad side crosscourt.

5.

Name: Volley to Baseline Warm-Up
Focus: Warm-up
Skill level: Intermediate, advanced
Setup: The player starts at the net on side B. The instructor starts at the baseline on side A.
Description: The player volleys back to the baseline to the instructor is many times he can without missing. The instructor hits every ball back to the player. The goal is to get to 20 shots in a row altogether.
Length: 5 min
Variation: The instructor can also play out the point against the player. The game ends when the player reaches 10 points.

6.

Name: Overhead Warm-up
Focus: Warm-up
Skill level: Intermediate, advanced
Setup: The player starts at the net on side B. The structure starts at the baseline on side A.
Description: The instructor feeds overheads to the player, who hits them back to the instructor with medium pace. The goal is to work together to reach 10 overheads in a row.
Length: 5 min
Variation: The player and the instructor can play out the point against each other. The instructor feeds an overhead but then can hit the ball anywhere on the court. The game ends when the player has 5 points.

7.

Name: Serve Warm-up
Focus: Warm-up
Skill level: Beginner, intermediate, advanced
Setup: The player starts at the baseline on side A. The instructor can position himself anywhere close to the player.
Description: The player keeps hitting first serves until he misses, then he hits a second serve. The goal is to get to 10 serves in a row. The player then switches to the ad side and repeats the drill.
Length: 10 min
Variation: The player can serve only first serves or only second serves.

8.

Name: Slice Warm-up
Focus: Warm-up
Skill level: Intermediate, advanced
Setup: Instructor starts on the deuce side on side A. The player starts in the middle of his baseline on side B.
Description: The instructor hits every ball to the player. The player can only hit slices back to the instructor. His goal is to reach 10 balls in a row. The drill is then repeated to the ad side. This is a great way to warm-up for volleys.
Length: 6-8 min
Variation: Beginners can try this drill from the T. They are not allowed to switch from the Continental grip.

Name: Lob Warm-up
Focus: Warm-up
Skill level: Intermediate, advanced
Setup: The instructor starts at the net position on side A. The player starts at the baseline on side B.
Description: The player tries to beat the instructor by hitting lobs over his head. The instructor hits every ball back to the player, and he is not allowed to step outside of the service boxes. The drill ends after the player wins 10 points.
Length: 5 min
Variation: For more advanced players the instructor can hit the ball wherever he wants to. In this variation the player can also hit passing shots.

10.

Name: Return Warm-up
Focus: Warm-up
Skill level: Beginner, intermediate, advanced
Setup: The instructor starts on the deuce side at the service line on side A. The player starts in return position on the deuce side on side B.
Description: The instructor hits serves from his service line right at the player who tries to block them back. After 10 successful returns, the instructor serves to the ad side.
Length: 5 min
Variation: For more advanced players the instructor can hit the ball further away from the player.

II.   *Ground strokes*

1.

Name: Control Drill
Focus: Ground strokes
Skill level: Intermediate, advanced
Setup: The player starts in the middle of his baseline slightly towards the deuce side. The instructor starts in the middle of his baseline.
Description: The player can hit the ball anywhere he wants, but the instructor can only hit the ball to the deuce side. Also, the player can only hit forehands (or backhands if he's left-handed). This is also true when the player comes forward to the net to hit volleys. The player tries to beat the instructor 10 times on the deuce side and 10 times on the ad side.
Length: 10-15 min

Variation: Lower level players can hit forehand or backhand volleys when they come to the net.

2.

Name: Passing Shot Drill
Focus: Ground strokes
Skill level: Intermediate, advanced
Setup: Both the instructor and the player starts in the middle of the baseline on the opposite sides.
Description: The instructor and the player start rallying from the baseline. The instructor attacks the net with every opportunity he gets. The player tries to win the point by hitting successful passing shots and lobs. The drill ends when the player gets 10 points.
Length: 8-10 min
Variation: The instructor can only hit the approach shot down the line against lower level players.

3.

Name: Directions Drill
Focus: Ground strokes
Skill level: Intermediate, advanced
Setup: Both the instructor and the player starts in the middle of the baseline on the opposite sides.
Description: The instructor and the player play out points against each other half-court in all four directions: deuce side cross court, ad side cross court, deuce side down the line, and ad side down the line. In each direction the player tries to beat the instructor five times.
Length: 15-25 min
Variation: Lower level players can also include the alleys in the drill.

4.

Name: Defense Drill
Focus: Ground strokes
Skill level: Intermediate, advanced
Setup: The instructor starts on the deuce side baseline on side A. The player starts in the middle of the baseline on side B.
Description: The player and the instructor start rallying. The instructor can hit the ball anywhere he wants to, but the player can only hit it back to the instructor on the deuce side. The instructor tries to hit a great variety of shots to the player. Also, he tries to make him run as much as possible. The player has to retrieve every ball and return it to the deuce side of the court. Once he returns 10 balls in a row, the drill is repeated from the ad side.

Length: 12-15 min
Variation: The player can hit volleys anywhere he wants to.

5.

Name: Change of Direction Drill
Focus: Ground strokes
Skill level: Intermediate, advanced
Setup: The instructor starts in the middle of the baseline on side A. The player starts in the middle of the baseline slightly towards the deuce side on side B.
Description: The player needs to hit one ball crosscourt and one ball down the line aiming only to half-court. The instructor needs to return every ball back to the player to the deuce side. The player can only hit forehands (or backhands if he's left-handed). Volleys are not allowed. Once a player scores 10 points against the instructor, the drill is repeated from the ad side.
Length: 12-15 min
Variation: Lower level players don't need to alternate their shots; they can hit the ball anywhere they want to.

6.

Name: Crosscourt Only Drill
Focus: Ground strokes
Skill level: Intermediate, advanced
Setup: Both the player and the instructor start at the opposite baselines in the middle.
Description: The instructor can hit the ball wherever he wants to. The player can only hit the ball crosscourt. Volleys can go anywhere. Once he scores 10 points against the instructor, the drill ends.
Length: 10-12 min
Variation: If the player decides to come to the net, he can also hit the approach shot anywhere he wants to.

7.

Name: Switch Drill
Focus: Ground strokes
Skill level: Intermediate, advanced
Setup: Both the player and the instructor start at the opposite baselines in the middle.
Description: The instructor and the player start rallying crosscourt on the deuce side. The instructor can only hit the ball crosscourt, but the player can decide to go down the line at any time. However, from that point on the instructor can also hit the ball anywhere he wants to. The goal is to win 10 points from the deuce side and the ad side.

Length: 12-15 min
Variation: The instructor can also switch down the line at any point. This is only recommended with advanced players.

8.

Name: Inside Out Drill
Focus: Ground strokes
Skill level: Advanced
Setup: Both the player and the instructor start at the opposite baselines in the middle.
Description: The instructor and the player start rallying crosscourt on the ad side (or the deuce side if the player is left-handed). Both the player and the instructor can only hit the ball crosscourt until the player decides to hit a forehand which he can hit anywhere he wants to. From that point both the instructor and the player can hit the ball wherever they want to. Player wins the drill when he collects 10 points.
Length: 8-12 min
Variation: The description assumes that the player has a better forehand. If his backhand is stronger, then the drill is reversed.

9.

Name: No man's Game
Focus: Ground strokes
Skill level: Advanced
Setup: The player and instructor both start at the opposite baselines.
Description: The instructor and the player start rallying, but they can only hit the ball into no man's land (between the service line and the baseline). Once a player wins 10 points, the drill ends.
Length: 7-9 min
Variation: More advanced players can play a game against instructor. The instructor also keeps his score.

10.

Name: Drop Shot Drill
Focus: Ground strokes
Skill level: Intermediate, advanced
Setup: The instructor starts at the baseline on the deuce side on side A. The player starts in the middle of the baseline on side B.
Description: The player and instructor start rallying. The player can only hit the ball back to the instructor. The instructor hits every ball close to the player. When the player has an opportunity, he can hit a drop shot to the ad side. From this point on, the instructor and the

player play out the point. After the player wins 5 points, the instructor moves to the ad side and the drill is repeated.

Length: 10-12 min

Variation: Hitting a drop shot that the instructor can not touch earns the player 2 points.

III. _Net approach_

1.

Name: Sudden Approach

Focus: Net approach

Skill level: Intermediate, advanced

Setup: Both the instructor and the player starts in the middle of the baseline on the opposite sides.

Description: The instructor feeds a short ball to either the deuce side or the ad side. The player must hit the approach shot down the line and come to the net. The instructor and the player play out the point against each other. The game ends when the player has 10 points.

Length: 10-12 min

Variation: Lower level players can hit the approach shot wherever they want.

2.

Name: Four Ball Drill

Focus: Net approach

Skill level: Intermediate, advanced

Setup: Both the player and the instructor start in the middle of the opposite baselines.

Description: The instructor and the player play out four points in rapid succession. The first ball is always a short ball, the second and third is always a volley, and the fourth is always an overhead. The player scores one point every time he wins the rally. After the four balls are played out, the player returns to his baseline and repeats the drill. Once a player reaches 15 points, the drill ends.

Length: 10-15 min

Variation: The instructor can also keep his score and try to reach 15 points.

3.

Name: "Short" Drill

Focus: Net approach

Skill level: Intermediate, advanced

Setup: The instructor starts on the deuce side baseline on side A. The player starts in the middle of the baseline on side B.

Description: The player and the instructor start rallying. The instructor can hit the ball anywhere he wants to, but the player can only hit it back to the instructor on the deuce side. At a random time the instructor will hit a short ball and yells out "short". From that point the player can also hit the ball wherever he wants to. He approaches the net and plays out the point against the instructor. Once he scores five points, the instructor moves to the ad side and the drill is repeated.
Length: 10-15 min
Variation: More advanced players can only hit the approach shot down the line.

4.

Name: Drop Drill
Focus: Net approach
Skill level: Intermediate, advanced
Setup: The instructor starts on the deuce side baseline on side A. The player starts in the middle of the baseline on side B.
Description: The player and the instructor start rallying. The instructor can hit the ball anywhere he wants to, but the player can only hit it back to the instructor on the deuce side. The instructor hits a drop shot when he gets an opportunity. From that point, the player can hit the ball wherever he wants to and the point is played out. Once a player wins five points, the instructor switches to the ad side and the drill is repeated.
Length: 8-10 min
Variation: For intermediate players the game can be changed where they can get one point for every drop shot they retrieve.

5.

Name: Invaders
Focus: Net approach
Skill level: Advanced
Setup: Both the player and the instructor start at the opposite baseline in the middle.
Description: The player and instructor immediately start playing out the point. Neither the instructor nor the player can come forward to the net until they receive a short ball into one of the service boxes. The person who received the short ball can come to the net at that point, however he doesn't have to. Winning a point with a volley is worth two points. The game ends when the player or the instructor reaches 15 points.
Length: 10-15 min
Variation: The instructor can not score 2 points against lower level players.

6.

Name: Chip and Charge
Focus: Net approach
Skill level: Intermediate, advanced
Setup: The instructor starts in deuce side serving position on side A. The player starts in deuce side returning position on side B.
Description: The instructor serves second serves only to the player. The player has to move forward and approach the net with a slice. The point is then played out. Once a player wins 10 points, the drill is repeated from the ad side.
Length: 10-15 min
Variation: The instructor is not allowed to hit topspin second serves against lower level players.

7.

Name: Doubles Approach
Focus: Net approach
Skill level: Intermediate, advanced
Setup: Both the instructor and the player start on the deuce side at the opposite baselines.
Description: The instructor and the player start rallying crosscourt on the deuce side. The doubles alleys are in. Once a player has the opportunity to come forward, he attacks the net and plays out the point against the instructor, still crosscourt. After he wins five points, the drill is repeated on the ad side.
Length: 10-15 min
Variation: The player can volley wherever he wants to.

8.

Name: Serve and Volley Drill
Focus: Net approach
Skill level: Intermediate, advanced
Setup: The instructor starts on the deuce side in returning position on side B. The player starts on side A on the deuce side in serving position.
Description: The player serves and approaches the net. The instructor returns the ball close to the player, so he has a chance to hit a volley. The point is played out. Once the player wins the point on the deuce side, he switches to the ad side. The drill ends when the player wins 10 points overall.
Length: 10-15 min
Variation: The instructor can keep his score against more advanced players. The player serves to the opposite side after each point.

Name: Serve and Volley Doubles
Focus: Net approach
Skill level: Intermediate, advanced
Setup: The player starts in doubles serving position on the deuce side on side A. The instructor starts in returning position on the deuce side on side B.
Description: The player serves and approaches the net. The instructor and the player play out the point crosscourt only. Doubles alleys are in. After the player wins five points, the drill is repeated on the ad side.
Length: 10-15 min
Variation: The player can volley wherever he wants to.

10.

Name: Split Step Drill
Focus: Net approach
Skill level: Intermediate, advanced
Setup: The player starts just behind the service line in the middle on side B. The instructor starts in the middle of the baseline on side A.
Description: The instructor drops the ball and feeds it after the bounce. The player can start coming forward when the instructor releases the ball. When the instructor makes contact with the ball in the feed, the player makes a split step. The point is played out and the game ends when the player wins 10 points against the instructor.
Length: 10-12 min
Variation: The instructor can feed the ball from the deuce or the ad side corner.

IV. *Net play*

1.

Name: Half-Court Volley Battle
Focus: Net play
Skill level: Intermediate, advanced
Setup: The player and the instructor start at the opposite service line on the right side of the court.
Description: The player and the instructor play out the point half-court down the line with alleys in. The game ends when the player wins five points against the instructor.
Length: 5-10 min
Variation: The game can also be played crosscourt on both sides.

2.

Name: Volley Bombardment
Focus: Net play
Skill level: Intermediate, advanced
Setup: The player starts in net position on side B. The instructor starts in the middle of the baseline on side A.
Description: The instructor feeds hard balls at the player in quick succession. The goal is to make 10 volleys back in a row.
Length: 5-10 min
Variation: For more advanced players the instructor can feed the ball from closer to the net.

3.

Name: No Bounce Drill
Focus: Net play
Skill level: Intermediate, advanced
Setup: The player starts in net position on side B. The instructor starts in the middle of the baseline on side A.
Description: The instructor feeds volleys and overheads to the player. The player is not allowed to let the ball bounce. The goal is to make 10 shots back in a row. If the ball bounces, the player has to start over.
Length: 5-10 min
Variation: The instructor and the player can play out the point. If the player lets the ball bounce, he loses the point. The game ends when the player wins 10 points against the instructor.

4.

Name: Overhead Points
Focus: Net play
Skill level: Beginner, intermediate, advanced
Setup: The player starts in net position on side B. The instructor starts in the middle of the baseline on side A.
Description: The instructor feeds a lob to the player and the point is played out. The game ends when the player wins 5 points in a row.
Length: 6-8 min
Variation: Beginners can play the game until they win 3 points in a row.

5.

Name: Drop Shot Volley Drill
Focus: Net play
Skill level: Intermediate, advanced
Setup: The player starts in net position on side B. The instructor starts in the middle of the baseline on side A.
Description: The instructor feeds balls straight to the player who is trying to hit drop shot volleys. The player is successful if the ball bounces twice before the service line on side A. The goal is to make 10 good drop shots in a row.
Length: 5-10 min
Variation: More advanced players can aim for three bounces before the service line.

6.

Name: Half Volley Drill
Focus: Net play
Skill level: Intermediate, advanced
Setup: The player starts at the service line on side B. The instructor starts in the middle of the baseline on side A.
Description: The instructor hits low balls only to the player's feet. The player has to return 10 balls in a row to win the game. After each shot, he has to go back to the service line. He can either move in and hit a volley, or he can let the ball bounce and hit half volley. The instructor's goal is to hit the ball just in front of the player, so he can hit a half volley.
Length: 5-10 min
Variation: The player can start from just behind the service line and move in right when the instructor starts feeding the ball. This way he has to hit a half volley while he's moving forward.

7.

Name: Change of Direction Volleys
Focus: Net play
Skill level: Intermediate, advanced
Setup: The player starts in a half-court net position on the ad side on side B. The instructor starts on the deuce side at the baseline on side A.
Description: The instructor feeds a ball to the player who has to volley it back to the instructor. The instructor returns the ball to the player who can now hit the ball crosscourt to the ad side. The player only hits two volleys each point: one down the line and one crosscourt. This drill simulates doubles play. The goal is to complete five points without a mistake. The drill is repeated from the opposite side of the court afterwards.
Length: 5-10 min

Variation: The player and the instructor can play out the points against each other. The player can not hit the ball crosscourt until the third shot. The goal is to win five points on each half.

8.

Name: Intimidation
Focus: Net play
Skill level: Intermediate, advanced
Setup: The player starts in a half-court net position on the ad side on side B. The instructor starts on the deuce side at the baseline on side A.
Description: The instructor and the player play out the point down the line half-court with alleys in. The instructor can only win the point with a volley, so he's trying to get closer and closer to the net with each shot. The player wins the game once he reaches 10 points.
Length: 8-10 min
Variation: The game can be played on full-court against beginner players. Since the instructor can only win the point with a volley, he needs to hit every ball back to the player and only put the volley away.

9.

Name: Swinging Volley Drill
Focus: Net play
Skill level: Intermediate, advanced
Setup: The player starts behind the service line on side B. The instructor starts in the middle of the baseline on side A.
Description: The instructor feeds a high ball the player who starts the point with the swinging volley. The point is played out and then repeated until the player wins 10 points.
Length: 8-10 min
Variation: More advanced players need to hit the first ball down the line.

10.

Name: Less Backswing Drill
Focus: Net play
Skill level: Beginner, intermediate, advanced
Setup: The player starts out with his back against the fence. The instructor starts about 10 feet from the player.
Description: The instructor and the player start volleying back and forth. They are working together to reach 15 volleys in a row. The ball can not bounce. At any point the player's back needs to be touching the back fence, so he can not take his racquet too far back for his volleys.

Length: 5-8 min
Variation: The instructor can back up further if the drill is too easy.

V.   *Serve and return*

1.

Name: Beat the Invisible Opponent
Focus: Serve
Skill level: Beginner, intermediate
Setup: The player starts at the baseline on the deuce side on side A. The instructor can position himself anywhere close to the player.
Description: The player plays out a whole game with only serves. He keeps score just like in a regular match. Obviously, he can only lose the point by hitting a double fault. Once a player wins the game, the drill is over.
Length: 4 min
Variation: More advanced players can try to beat this drill by having only one serve per point.

2.

Name: Serves In a Row
Focus: Serve
Skill level: Beginner, intermediate, advanced
Setup: The player starts at the baseline on the deuce side on side A. The instructor can position himself anywhere close to the player.
Description: The player tries to hit as many serves in as possible in a row. The second bounce of the serve needs to be behind the baseline or outside the doubles sideline. The player's goal is to reach 10 serves in a row.
Length: 10-12 min
Variation: The second bounce rule does not apply for beginner players.

3.

Name: Serve Placement
Focus: Serve
Skill level: Beginner, intermediate, advanced
Setup: The player starts at the baseline on the deuce side on side A. The instructor can position himself anywhere close to the player.
Description: The instructor places a line of balls in the middle of both service boxes dividing them into two halves each. The player tries to hit each half one after another from left to

right. Then go back from right to left. Any time the player misses, he has to start over.
Length: 10-15 min
Variation: For more advanced players the instructor can divide the service boxes into thirds.

4.

Name: Target Practice
Focus: Serve
Skill level: Beginner, intermediate, advanced
Setup: The player starts at the baseline on the deuce side on side A. The instructor places two targets in each service boxes. One target goes to every corner of the service boxes. The targets can be anything from a ball to a basket. The instructor can position himself anywhere close to the player.
Description: The player has to hit each target from left to right. Once he hits a target, you can move on to the next one. After the last target on the right is hit, the targets are set up again and the player tries to hit them from right to left this time.
Length: 15-30 min
Variation: Beginner players can have bigger targets.

5.

Name: Right or Left Drill
Focus: Serve
Skill level: Beginner, intermediate, advanced
Setup: The player starts at the baseline on the deuce side on side A. The instructor starts in returning position on the deuce side on side B.
Description: The goal of the player is to hit 10 balls to the instructor's forehand and 10 more to his backhand. The instructor is not allowed to move and he doesn't return the ball. The ball simply has to pass him from the correct side. Once the deuce side is complete, the player and the instructor switch to the ad side and repeat the drill.
Length: 15-25 min
Variation: With more advanced players the instructor can try to reach the ball. He's still not allowed to move, but if he returns the ball, the serve does not count.

6.

Name: Power Serve
Focus: Serve
Skill level: Beginner, intermediate, advanced
Setup: The player starts at the baseline on the deuce side on side A. The instructor can position himself anywhere close to the player.
Description: The player hits a serve and counts how many times the ball bounces before

it reaches the back fence. It tries to minimize the number of bounces by hitting the serve as hard as he can. Two or three bounces are acceptable, depending on how far the back fence is. The player then serves to the ad side.
Length: 5-10 min
Variation: Advanced players can try to hit the back fence on the second bounce.

7.

Name: Volleyball Serve
Focus: Serve
Skill level: Intermediate, advanced
Setup: The instructor ties a rope about a foot above the net in between the two net posts. The player starts at the baseline on the deuce side on side A. The instructor can position himself anywhere close to the player.
Description: The player tries to hit topspin serves above the rope into the service box. His goal is to reach 10 serves in a row. The player then repeats the drill to the ad side.
Length: 5-10 min
Variation: The instructor can place the rope a little higher for more advanced players.

8.

Name: Reflex Returns
Focus: Return
Skill level: Beginner, intermediate, advanced
Setup: The instructor starts at the service line on the deuce side on side A. The player starts in returning position on the deuce side on side B.
Description: The instructor hits serves right at the player fairly hard. The player has to return the serves anyway he can. Once he returned 20 balls, they switch to the ad side.
Length: 10-12 min
Variation: More advanced players need to return 10 balls crosscourt and 10 balls down the line.

9.

Name: Deep Returns
Focus: Return
Skill level: Intermediate, advanced
Setup: The instructor starts at the baseline on the deuce side on side A. The player starts in returning position on the deuce side on side B.
Description: The instructor hits first and second serves. The player tries to collect 15 points. He gets two points if he returns the ball between the service line and the baseline. He gets one point if he returns the ball into one of the service boxes. He loses a point if he misses

the return. Once the player reaches 15 points, the drill is repeated from the ad side.
Length: 10-12 min
Variation: More advanced players get zero points if they return the ball into one of the service boxes.

10.

Name: First Shot Drill
Focus: Serve
Skill level: Advanced
Setup: The player starts at the baseline on the deuce side on side A. The instructor starts in returning position on the deuce side on side B.
Description: The player starts the point by serving first serves only. The instructor blocks the ball back to the middle of the court. The point is then played out. It is up to the player if he attacks the net or not. The player needs to win 10 points on both sides.
Length: 15-20 min
Variation: If the player hits a winner on the first shot, he gets two points.

VI.   Footwork

1.

Name: Drop Shot Run
Focus: Footwork
Skill level: Intermediate, advanced
Setup: Both the instructor and the player starts in the middle of the baseline on the opposite sides.
Description: The instructor and the player start rallying from the baseline. At the random time the instructor hits a drop shot. From that point the player and the instructor can hit the ball wherever they want. The player tries to win five points against the instructor.
Length: 8-10 min
Variation: Lower level players can score a point by simply returning the drop shot.

2.

Name: Side to Side Short Drill
Focus: Footwork
Skill level: Beginner, intermediate, advanced
Setup: The player and the instructor both start at the T on opposite sides.
Description: The instructor feeds one ball left and one ball right. The player needs to hit a down the line shot on both sides. The player gets a point after each successful shot and

loses a point if he doesn't get to a ball. His goal is to reach 20 points. The drill is then repeated with cross courts.

Length: 10-15 min

Variation: The instructor can place targets on the deuce and the ad side. If the player hits the target, he scores two points.

3.

Name: Side to Side Short (random) Drill

Focus: Footwork

Skill level: Beginner, intermediate, advanced

Setup: The player and the instructor both start at the T on opposite sides.

Description: The instructor feeds short balls in a random order. The player needs to hit a down the line shot on both sides. The player gets a point after each successful shot and loses a point if he doesn't get to a ball. The goal is to reach 20 points. The drill is then repeated with cross courts.

Length: 10-15 min

Variation: The instructor can place targets on the deuce and the ad side. If the player hits the target, he scores two points.

4.

Name: Side to Side Drill

Focus: Footwork

Skill level: Beginner, intermediate, advanced

Setup: The player starts at the baseline in the middle on side B. The instructor feeds from the T on side A.

Description: The instructor feeds one ball left and one ball right. The player needs to hit a down the line shot on both sides. The player gets a point after each successful shot and loses a point if he doesn't get to a ball. His goal is to reach 20 points. The drill is then repeated with cross courts.

Length: 10-15 min

Variation: The instructor can place targets on the deuce and the ad side. If the player hits the target, he scores two points.

5.

Name: Side to Side (random) Drill

Focus: Footwork

Skill level: Beginner, intermediate, advanced

Setup: The player starts at the baseline in the middle on side B. The instructor feeds from the T on side A.

Description: The instructor feeds balls to the player in a random order. The player needs to hit a down the line shot on both sides. The player gets a point after each successful shot and loses a point if he doesn't get to a ball. The goal is to reach 20 points. The drill is then repeated with cross courts.
Length: 10-15 min
Variation: The instructor can place targets on the deuce and the ad side. If the player hits the target, he scores two points.

6.

Name: Inside Forehands
Focus: Footwork
Skill level: Intermediate, advanced
Setup: The player starts at the baseline in the middle on side B. The instructor feeds from the T on side A. A target is set up on the deuce side on side A.
Description: The instructor feeds one ball to the player's forehand and one to the middle. The player has to hit both balls with a forehand aiming at the target. He has to run around the middle ball to hit a forehand by all means. Once he hits the target, it is moved to the ad side. The drill ends when the player hits the target on the ad side.
Length: 5-10 min
Variation: If a player has a better backhand (which is rare), the drill is reversed so the player can hit backhands.

7.

Name: Suicide Drill
Focus: Footwork
Skill level: Beginner, intermediate, advanced
Setup: The player starts at the baseline in the middle on side B. The instructor feeds from the T on side A.
Description: The instructor feeds balls to every possible place on the court. The player has to let each ball bounce. The instructor can get very creative with his feeds hitting anything from low slices to high top spins. The goal is to return 20 balls in a row. If the player misses, it has to start over.
Length: 10-12 min
Variation: The drill can be played for a specific time. For example, the player has to return balls for 1 min.

8.

Name: Side to Side Volley Drill
Focus: Footwork

Skill level: Beginner, intermediate, advanced

Setup: The player starts at the net on side B. The instructor feeds from the baseline on side A.

Description: The instructor feeds one ball left and one ball right. The player needs to volley down the line on both sides. The player gets a point after each successful volley and loses a point if he doesn't get to a ball. His goal is to reach 20 points. The drill is then repeated with cross court volleys.

Length: 10-15 min

Variation: The instructor can mix in an overhead from time to time.

9.

Name: Side to Side Volley (random) Drill

Focus: Footwork

Skill level: Beginner, intermediate, advanced

Setup: The player starts at the net on side B. The instructor feeds from the baseline on side A.

Description: The instructor feeds balls to the player in a random order. The player needs to volley down the line on both sides. The player gets a point after each successful volley and loses a point if he doesn't get to a ball. The goal is to reach 20 points. The drill is then repeated with cross courts.

Length: 10-15 min

Variation: The instructor can mix in an overhead from time to time.

10.

Name: Four Shot Drill

Focus: Footwork

Skill level: Beginner, intermediate, advanced

Setup: The player starts at the baseline in the middle on side B. The instructor feeds from the T on side A.

Description: The instructor feeds four balls to the player: one deep forehand, one short backhand, a forehand volley, and an overhead. The balls are fed in a way where the player needs to run them down. Once the player completes three perfect rounds, the drill is reversed.

Length: 10-12 min

Variation: The instructor can place targets around the court. If the player hits the target, that round will count as a perfect round.

Semi-private Lessons

This section includes two player lessons with an instructor. It is a fairly common practice since many times friends feel comfortable taking lessons together. The instructor often participates in these drills as a third player. One obvious setup for the players is to play games against each other. Even though some of the drills are played out this way, it is not recommended for every situation. Many times players, especially friends, feel uncomfortable playing competitively against each other. The best way to find out if this indeed is the case is to try one drill and get some feedback from the players. If they liked it, the instructor can move on to the next drill. If one of them gets frustrated, the instructor can choose different drills and ask them time to time if they are ready for competitive play. Still semi-private lessons provide a great balance between instruction and fun.

I. *Warm-up*

1.

Name: No-Man's Land Drill
Focus: Warm-up
Skill level: Intermediate, advanced
Setup: Players start at the opposite baselines. The instructor feeds from the net post.
Description: The instructor feeds the ball in to one of the players. Players start rallying and earn points every time they hit the ball between the service line and the baseline. The instructor calls out the score after each successful shot. The service line is in. Players can not volley; they have to let every ball bounce. The first player to 30 points is the winner. This is a great warm-up drill.
Length: 8-10 min
Variation: Players can score an extra point every time they win the point.

2.

Name: In and Out
Focus: Warm-up
Skill level: Intermediate, advanced
Setup: Players start at the opposite baselines in the middle. The instructor feeds the ball from the net post.
Description: The players are working together in this drill. As the rally continues, players try to get closer and closer to the net until they hit really short volleys to each other. Then they

try to work their way back to the baseline while keeping the ball in play. If a shot is missed, the players have to start over. Completing a full in and out is worth one point. The goal is to set a record.

Length: 5-10 min

Variation: Advanced players can limit rounds by hitting exactly 2 ground strokes 2 volleys in and 2 volleys 2 ground strokes out.

3.

Name: Baseline Triangle

Focus: Warm-up

Skill level: Intermediate, advanced

Setup: The instructor starts at the baseline on the deuce side on side A. The players start on side B with one of them on each side at the baseline.

Description: The instructor hits one ball crosscourt and one ball down the line. Doubles alleys are out. The players return every ball back to the instructor's side. The instructor and the players are working together to reach 20 shots in a row. Players switch sides after the 20 shots. The drill is then repeated from the ad side.

Length: 8-10 min

Variation: The game can be played where the doubles alleys count as in.

4.

Name: Baseline Volley Triangle

Focus: Warm-up

Skill level: Intermediate, advanced

Setup: The instructor starts on the deuce side at the baseline on side A. The players start at the net on side B with one on each side.

Description: The instructor hits one ball crosscourt and one ball down the line. Doubles alleys are out. The players volley every ball back to the instructor's side. The instructor and the players are working together to reach 20 shots in a row. Players switch sides after the 20 shots. The drill is then repeated from the ad side.

Length: 8-10 min

Variation: The game can be played where the doubles alleys count as in.

5.

Name: Volley Triangle

Focus: Warm-up

Skill level: Intermediate, advanced

Setup: The instructor starts on the deuce side at the service line on side A. The players start at the net on side B with one on each side.

Description: The instructor volleys one ball crosscourt and one ball down the line. Doubles alleys are out. The players return every ball back to the instructor's side. The instructor and the players are working together to reach 20 volleys in a row. Players switch sides after the 20 shots. The drill is then repeated from the ad side.
Length: 8-10 min
Variation: The game can be played where the doubles alleys count as in.

6.

Name: Overhead Triangle
Focus: Warm-up
Skill level: Intermediate, advanced
Setup: The instructor starts on the deuce side at the baseline on side A. The players start at the net on side B with one on each side.
Description: The instructor feeds one lob crosscourt and one lob down the line. Doubles alleys are out. The players hit every overhead back to the instructor's side. The instructor and the players are working together to reach 20 volleys in a row. Players switch sides after the 20 shots. The drill is then repeated from the ad side.
Length: 8-10 min
Variation: The game can be played where the doubles alleys count as in.

7.

Name: Volley to Ground Strokes Co-op
Focus: Warm-up
Skill level: Intermediate, advanced
Setup: One player starts at the net on side A. The other player starts at the baseline on side B. The instructor feeds the ball from side A.
Description: The instructor feeds the ball in and the players start rallying back to each other. The goal is to reach 20 shots in a row without a mistake. The roles are reversed afterwards.
Length: 8-10 min
Variation: More advanced players can hit the volleys behind the service line only. This way they only need to get to 10 shots in a row.

8.

Name: Overhead Warm-Up Co-op
Focus: Warm-up
Skill level: Intermediate, advanced
Setup: One player starts at the net on side A. The other player starts at the baseline on side B. The instructor feeds the ball from side A.
Description: The instructor feeds the ball in and the baseline player hits a lob. The net play-

er returns the ball with an overhead. The drill continues with lobs and overheads until the two players get to 20 shots in a row without a mistake. The roles are reversed afterwards.
Length: 8-10 min
Variation: To make the game easier, the net player can let the overhead bounce.

9.

Name: Mini Tennis Warm-up
Focus: Warm-up
Skill level: Intermediate, advanced
Setup: Players start at the opposite service lines at the T. The instructor feeds the ball from the net post.
Description: The instructor feeds a low ball to a random side. The players play out the point by hitting only into the service boxes. They can hit the ball any way they want to. The game goes to 10 points.
Length: 5-8 min
Variation: Beginners can play the game in only one service box.

10.

Name: Volley to Volley Co-op
Focus: Warm-up
Skill level: Intermediate, advanced
Setup: Players start at the opposite service lines at the T. The instructor feeds the ball from side A.
Description: The instructor feeds the ball in and the players start volleying back and forth. The goal is to reach 20 volleys in a row without a mistake.
Length: 5-8 min
Variation: More advanced players need to alternate one forehand and one backhand volley. If they miss the order, they must start over.

II.   *Ground strokes*

1.

Name: Master and Servant
Focus: Ground strokes
Skill level: Intermediate, advanced
Setup: Both players start at their baseline in the middle. The player on side B is the "master"; the player on side A is the "servant". The instructor feeds the ball from side A.
Description: The instructor feeds the ball to the deuce side on side B. The player on side B

has to hit one shot to the deuce side and one to the ad side. The "servant" has to return every ball to the deuce side. Only half courts count on both sides. The first player to 15 points wins a round. Switch roles after each round and also play the ad sides.
Length: 15-25 min
Variation: Include the doubles alleys for more running.

2.

Name: Butterfly Drill
Focus: Ground strokes
Skill level: Intermediate, advanced
Setup: Both players start at their baseline in the middle. The instructor feeds the ball from side A.
Description: The player on side B can only hit crosscourt while the player on side A can only hit down the line. Only half courts are in. Play to 10 points then reverse the roles. Play continues to 21 points.
Length: 10-15 min
Variation: The down the line hitting player gets 2 points every time since he has to run more.

3.

Name: Alley Rally (Down the Line)
Focus: Ground strokes
Skill level: Intermediate, advanced
Setup: One player starts on deuce side on side A, the other player starts on ad side on side B. The instructor feeds the ball from the ad side on side A.
Description: Players rally down the line and score points every time they hit the ball in the doubles alley. Players switch sides after score reaches 15 points and continue until 30.
Length: 10-15 min
Variation: To even the game, make players hit only forehand to forehand or backhand to backhand in each round.

4.

Name: Alley Rally (Crosscourt)
Focus: Ground strokes
Skill level: Intermediate, advanced
Setup: Both players start on the deuce side at opposite sides. The instructor feeds the ball from the ad side on side A.
Description: Players rally crosscourt and score points every time they hit the ball in the doubles alley. Players switch to the ad side after score reaches 15 points. The instructor

switches and feeds from the deuce side on side A. Play continues until one player reaches 30 points.

Length: 10-15 min

Variation: For more challenge make players alternate forehands and backhands.

5.

Name: Topspin – Slice Drill

Focus: Ground strokes

Skill level: Intermediate, advanced

Setup: Both players start at their baseline in the middle. The instructor feeds the ball from the net post.

Description: The instructor feeds the ball in to a random player. The point is played out but the players have to alternate topspin and slice shots. To make the game even, the instructor has to alternate feeding the ball to each side. The first player to reach 15 points is the winner.

Length: 10-12 min

Variation: One player hits only topspin and the other one only slice.

6.

Name: Switch Drill

Focus: Ground strokes

Skill level: Intermediate, advanced

Setup: Both players start at their baseline in the middle. The instructor feeds the ball from side A. The player on side B is the switcher.

Description: The instructor feeds the ball to the ad side. The players start hitting backhand crosscourt on half-court. The player on side A can only hit crosscourt. The switcher on side B can switch down the line at any time. After the switch, both players can hit the ball wherever they want to. The game continues to 20 points; the players switch sides at 10 points.

Length: 10-15 min

Variation: The drill can also be played from the opposite side.

7.

Name: Four Directions Drill

Focus: Ground strokes

Skill level: Intermediate, advanced

Setup: Both players start at their baseline in the middle. The instructor feeds the ball from side A.

Description: The instructor feeds the ball into the deuce side. The players play out the point crosscourt. Doubles alleys are out. Play continues to 10 points. The drill is repeated to the opposite crosscourt and then the two down the line directions. Play each direction to 10 points.

Length: 25-30 min

Variation: Doubles alleys can be in for doubles practice.

8.

Name: Triangle Game

Focus: Ground strokes

Skill level: Intermediate, advanced

Setup: Both players start on side B at the baseline with one player on the deuce side and the other one on the ad side. The instructor starts on side A at the baseline on the deuce side.

Description: Both players start with 10 points each. The instructor hits one ball crosscourt and one ball down the line half-court only. The players need to return every ball back to the instructor side. If the players miss, they lose the point. The player that survives longer is the winner. Players switch sides after each round. The instructor switches sides after the second round.

Length: 18-20 min

Variation: The instructor can also keep his points.

9.

Name: Fast Triangle Game

Focus: Ground strokes

Skill level: Intermediate, advanced

Setup: Both players start on side B at the baseline with one player on the deuce side and the other one on the ad side. The instructor starts on side A at the net on the deuce side.

Description: Both players start with 10 points each. The instructor volleys one ball cross-court and one ball down the line half-court only. The players need to return every ball back to the instructor side. If the players miss, they lose the point. The player that survives longer is the winner. Players switch sides after each round. The instructor switches sides after the second round.

Length: 18-20 min

Variation: The instructor can also keep his points.

10.

Name: Side to Side Recovery Drill

Focus: Ground strokes

Skill level: Intermediate, advanced

Setup: One player starts on side B at the baseline in the middle. The instructor and the second player start at the baseline on side A. The instructor starts on the deuce side; the player starts on the ad side.

Description: The instructor and the players can only hit the ball half-court. Side A can only hit the ball crosscourt; the player on side B can only hit the ball down the line. Around ends after a side reaches 10 points. After the first round, the instructor and the player on side A switch sides. After the second round, the players switch sides. The instructor and the players repeat the drill until both players have hit from every position.

Length: 25-30 min

Variation: If the player on side B is having trouble recovering the crosscourt shots, the directions can be switched where he is hitting the crosscourt.

III. *Net approach*

1.

Name: Singles Attack
Focus: Net approach
Skill level: Intermediate, advanced
Setup: Both players start at their baseline in the middle. The player on side B is the attacker; the player on side A is the defender. The instructor feeds the ball from side A.
Description: The instructor feeds a short ball into one of the service boxes. The attacker hits an approach shot and plays out the point. Both players can use any type of shots. The first player to 20 points wins the game. Players switch roles when the score reaches 10 points.
Length: 12-15 min
Variation: If the defender has a hard time returning the first shot, make the attacker hit the approach shot down the line.

2.

Name: Ruler of the Net
Focus: Net approach
Skill level: Intermediate, advanced
Setup: Both players start at their baseline in the middle. The instructor feeds the ball from the net post.
Description: The instructor feeds the ball in to a random player. The players rally and play out the points. They score two points if they win the point with a volley. The game ends when a player reaches 21 points.
Length: 10-12 min
Variation: Players have to let the first ball bounce on both sides to make it harder to come to the net immediately.

3.

Name: Doubles Approach
Focus: Net approach
Skill level: Intermediate, advanced
Setup: One player starts at the baseline on side B on the deuce side. The instructor starts at the service line on side A on the ad side. The second player starts at the baseline on side A on the deuce side.
Description: The instructor and his partner can only hit the ball to the player on the deuce side half-court. The instructor feeds a short ball to the player on side B who approaches the net. The point is played out and the game continues until one side reaches 10 points. After each round the players switch sides. After the second round, the drill is reversed where the player on side B and the instructor starts on the ad side.
Length: 15-20 min
Variation: The drill can be modified where the instructor can hit the ball wherever he wants to.

4.

Name: "Short" Drill
Focus: Net approach
Skill level: Intermediate, advanced
Setup: Both players start at their baseline in the middle. The instructor feeds the ball from the net post.
Description: The instructor feeds the ball to a random player. Players are only allowed to come to the net if their opponent hits the ball into one of the service boxes. When a short ball is hit, the instructor yells "short" and from that point the player can hit volleys. If the other player receives a short ball, he's also allowed to hit volleys. Any player that wins the point with a volley scores two points. The game ends when a player reaches 21 points.
Length: 12-15 min
Variation: Only the first player that receives a short ball can score 2 points with a volley.

5.

Name: Swinging Volley Drill
Focus: Net approach
Skill level: Intermediate, advanced
Setup: Both players start at their baseline in the middle. The instructor feeds the ball from side A.
Description: The instructor feeds a high ball to the player on side B. As the instructor starts the feed, the player on side B starts coming forward immediately, hits the ball with the swinging volley and approaches the net. The point is played out and the drill continues until

one player reaches 15 points. The roles are reversed after a round.
Length: 8-10 min
Variation: More advanced players need to hit the swinging volley down the line.

6.

Name: One Bounce Drill
Focus: Net approach
Skill level: Intermediate, advanced
Setup: Both players start at their baseline in the middle. The instructor feeds the ball from the net post.
Description: The instructor feeds a deep ball to a random player. The players have to let the first ball bounce, but after that no more bounces are allowed. Players have to rush to the net and hit volleys are overheads. If the ball bounces on their side the second time, they lose the point. The play continues until one player reaches 15 points.
Length: 10-15 min
Variation: The drill can be modified to a "two bounce drill" where the ball can bounce a second time during a point.

7.

Name: Serve and Volley Singles Game
Focus: Net approach
Skill level: Intermediate, advanced
Setup: One player starts in a serving position on side A; the other player in returning position on side B both on the deuce side. The instructor observes from the net post.
Description: The player on side A serves the ball and approaches the net. The point is played out freely. The second point is played from the ad side and so on. Players switch roles when the score reaches 10 points. The game ends at 21 points.
Length: 8-10 min
Variation: To make the drill easier for the server, he can hit as many serves as needed.

8.

Name: Serve and Volley Doubles Game
Focus: Net approach
Skill level: Intermediate, advanced
Setup: One player starts in a doubles serving position on side A; the other player in returning position on side B both on the deuce side. The instructor observes from the net post.
Description: The player on side A serves the ball and approaches the net. The point is played out crosscourt half-court only. Doubles alleys are in. Players switch roles when the score reaches 10 points. A round ends at 21 points. The players then switch to the ad side

and repeat the drill.

Length: 8-10 min

Variation: To make the drill easier for the server, he can hit as many serves as needed.

9.

Name: Chip and Charge Drill

Focus: Net approach

Skill level: Intermediate, advanced

Setup: One player starts in a serving position on side A; the other player in returning position on side B both on the deuce side. The instructor observes from the net post.

Description: The player on side a serves second serve. The player side B takes the return on the rise and attacks the net. Each point the server has only one serve. The second point is played from the ad side and so on. Players switch roles when the score reaches 10 points. The game ends at 21 points.

Length: 12-15 min

Variation: If the receiver has too much trouble returning the second serve, the instructor can serve the ball in play and quickly get out of the way.

10.

Name: Doubles Attack

Focus: Net approach

Skill level: Intermediate, advanced

Setup: Both players start on side B at the baseline with one player on the deuce side and the other on the ad side. The instructor starts on side A at the baseline in the middle.

Description: The instructor hits a short ball anywhere onto side B. The players work together as a team and attack the net. The players can only hit the ball within the singles sidelines. The points are played out until one side reaches 15 points. The drill can be repeated with the players on opposite sides.

Length: 12-15 min

Variation: Beginner players can hit the ball into the doubles alleys also.

IV.   *Net play*

1.

Name: 10 Volley Drill

Focus: Net play

Skill level: Beginner, intermediate, advanced

Setup: Both players start at the net on side B. The instructor feeds balls from the deuce side baseline on side A.

Description: The instructor feeds passing shots and lobs to the team. Their goal is to make 10 balls back in a row without a mistake.

Length: 3-5 min

Variation: The instructor can feed the balls from the middle or the ad side baseline.

2.

Name: Singles Volley Battle

Focus: Net play

Skill level: Intermediate, advanced

Setup: Both players start on the T on opposite sides. The instructor feeds the ball from side B.

Description: The instructor feeds the ball in to the player on side B. The point is then played out on the singles court. The players switch sides after the score reaches 10 points. The game ends when either player reaches 21 points.

Length: 8-10 min

Variation: The instructor can feed the ball to the players' feet to make the first ball a little harder.

3.

Name: Doubles Volley Battle

Focus: Net play

Skill level: Intermediate, advanced

Setup: Both players are at the service line on the deuce side on opposite sides. The instructor feeds the ball from side A.

Description: The instructor feeds the ball in to the player on side B. The point is played out crosscourt on the deuce side half-court only. Doubles alleys are in. The players switch after the score has reached 10 points. The game ends when either player reaches 21 points.

Length: 8-10 min

Variation: This game can be played from the opposite crosscourt side or even down the line.

4.

Name: Volley to Ground Stroke Drill (singles)

Focus: Net play

Skill level: Intermediate, advanced

Setup: One player is at the baseline in the middle on side B. The other player is at the net on side A. The instructor feeds the ball from side A.

Description: The instructor feeds the ball to the baseline player. The point is then played out on the singles court. The players switch sides at 10 points. The game continues until one of the players reach 21 points.
Length: 10-12 min
Variation: The instructor can feed the ball to either the forehand or backhand corner to make the first shot a little harder.

5.

Name: Volley to Ground Stroke Drill (doubles)
Focus: Net play
Skill level: Intermediate, advanced
Setup: One player is at the baseline on the deuce side on side B. The other player is at the net on the deuce side on side A. The instructor feeds the ball from side A.
Description: The instructor feeds the ball to the baseline player. The point is played out crosscourt, half-court only on the deuce side. Doubles alleys are in. The players switch sides at 10 points. The game continues until one of the players reach 21 points.
Length: 10-12 min
Variation: This game can be played from the opposite crosscourt side or even down the line.

6.

Name: Overhead Defense
Focus: Net play
Skill level: Intermediate, advanced
Setup: One player is at the net on side B. The other player is at the baseline on side A. The instructor feeds from side A.
Description: The instructor feeds a lob to the net player, so the point starts with an overhead. The point is played out on the singles court. The players switch positions after the score reaches 10 points. The game continues until a player reaches 21 points.
Length: 10-12 min
Variation: The instructor can hit higher lobs, so the player has to let it bounce before he hits the overhead.

7.

Name: Side to Side Volleys
Focus: Net play
Skill level: Intermediate, advanced
Setup: Both players start at the T on the opposite sides. The instructor feeds the ball from side A.

Description: The players work together in this drill. They need to keep the ball in the air with volleys. They also need to keep moving from one singles sideline to the other singles sideline as they keep volleying back and forth. If they miss or the ball bounces, they have to start over. The goal is to complete the round from one singles side line to the other.
Length: 8-10 min
Variation: More advanced players need to alternate forehand and backhand volleys. If they miss the order, they have to restart.

8.

Name: Volley Race
Focus: Net play
Skill level: Beginner, intermediate
Setup: The instructor places a number of balls along the middle service line about a foot apart. Both players are in the net on side B. One player is on the deuce side and the other player on the ad side. They both line up with the closest ball to the net. The instructor feeds from the T on side A.
Description: The instructor feeds one ball to each player. If a player makes the volley, he backs up to the next ball. If he misses the volley, he moves forward to the closest available ball. The player that reaches the service line first is the winner.
Length: 5-7 min
Variation: Beginner players do not have to move forward if they miss the ball.

9.

Name: Overhead Target Practice
Focus: Net play
Skill level: Beginner, intermediate
Setup: The instructor places a target on the T on side A. Both players start at the net on side B with one on the deuce side and the other on the ad side. The instructor feeds the ball from the baseline on side A.
Description: The instructor feeds one lob to each player. The players try to hit the target. They each get 20 chances then switch sides and 20 more. The player with the most hits wins the game.
Length: 6-8 min
Variation: The instructor can set up two targets: one on the deuce side and one on the ad site.

Name: Lob Tracking Drill
Focus: Net play
Skill level: Intermediate, advanced
Setup: Both players start at the net on opposite sides. The instructor feeds the ball from side A.
Description: The instructor feeds the deep lob to the net player on side B. The goal is to hit a deep enough lob where the player has to let it bounce. The player is allowed to hit the feed in the air, but if he can't, he has to run it down and play out the point that way. After 20 points the roles are reversed. The game ends after 20 more points.
Length: 10-12 min
Variation: The rules can be changed where the feed must bounce first.

V. *Serve and return*

1.

Name: Serve and Return Point Game
Focus: Serve and return
Skill level: Intermediate, advanced
Setup: One player starts on the deuce side serving position on side A. The other player starts on the deuce side returning position on side B. The instructor observes from the net post.
Description: The server hits first serves, and when he misses, hits second serves. The receiver tries to return the serve as deep as possible. The server scores one point any time his first serve is not returned. He also scores one point if his second serve is returned into one of the service boxes. He scores two points if his second serve is not returned at all. The receiver scores two points if he returns a first serve behind the service line and one point if he returns it into one of the service boxes. He also scores one point if he returns the second serve behind the service line. The roles are reversed at eight points. The server loses a point every time he hits a double fault. The first player to reach 15 points is the winner.
Length: 10-12 min
Variation: Players can place targets into the service box. Hitting them would give the server three points.

2.

Name: Serving Battle
Focus: Serve and return
Skill level: Beginner, intermediate, advanced

Setup: One player starts in serving position on the deuce side, the other on the ad side on side A. The instructor observes from behind the players.

Description: The players hit serves one by one. Every good serve is one point. The players switch sides at five points. The first player to reach 10 points is the winner. The winner has to win by two points.

Length: 5-10 min

Variation: More advanced players can try to hit 10 serves in a row. Any time they miss, they go back to zero.

3.

Name: Directional Returns

Focus: Serve and return

Skill level: Intermediate, advanced

Setup: One player starts on the deuce side serving position on side A. The other player starts on the deuce side returning position on side B. The instructor observes from the net post.

Description: After the player on side A serves, the return must go back to the deuce side half-court only. The point is then played out on the singles court. To the next point is played from the ad side. In that case the return goes back to the ad side. Each player serves 10 points and the player with the most points wins the game.

Length: 15-20 min

Variation: The game can be played with down the line returns also.

4.

Name: Deep Return Drill

Focus: Serve and return

Skill level: Intermediate, advanced

Setup: One player starts on the deuce side serving position on side A. The other player starts on the deuce side returning position on side B. The instructor observes from the net post.

Description: The player on side A hits only first serves. He scores a point if his serve is not returned. The receiver scores a point if he can return the serve behind the service line. If his return bounces in one of the service boxes, the point is played out on the singles court. Players switch between deuce and ad sides after each point. The game continues to 15 points then the roles are reversed.

Length: 18-20 min

Variation: Advanced players can hit second serves also.

5.

Name: Second Serve Attack
Focus: Serve and return
Skill level: Intermediate, advanced
Setup: One player starts on the deuce side serving position on side A. The other player starts on the deuce side returning position on side B. The instructor observes from the net post.
Description: The player on side A hits only second serves. If the receiver wins the point with the return, he receives two points. If the return is missed, the server gets two points. Players switch roles after one of them has reached 15 points. The game ends at 30 points.
Length: 18-20 min
Variation: To make the game easier for the receiver, missed returns are only worth one point.

6.

Name: Ace Game
Focus: Serve and return
Skill level: Intermediate, advanced
Setup: One player starts on the deuce side serving position on side A. The other player starts on the deuce side returning position on side B. The instructor observes from the net post.
Description: The player on side A only hits first serves. He only gets a point if his serve is not returned. If he hits an ace, he scores two points. Each player serves 20 balls. The player with the most points is the winner.
Length: 8-10 min
Variation: Aces can be worth three points.

7.

Name: Line Serving
Focus: Serve and return
Skill level: Advanced
Setup: Both players are in serving position on side A, one on the deuce side and one on the ad side. The instructor observes from side B.
Description: The players alternate serves. Their goal is to hit any lines surrounding the correct service box. When the instructor sees a hit, he awards one point to the appropriate server. Each server has 20 chances to score points. The player with the most points wins the game.
Length: 5-8 min
Variation: Players can aim only to a specific line such as the middle service line or the

single sidelines.

8.

Name: Quick Return Drill
Focus: Serve and return
Skill level: Intermediate, advanced
Setup: One player starts on the deuce side service line on side A. The other player starts on the deuce side returning position on side B. The instructor observes from the net post.
Description: The player on side A serves the ball from the service line. He has one chance to get the ball in. The ball is then played out on the singles court. The server hits 10 balls to the deuce side and 10 more to the ad side. The roles are then reversed. The player with the most points wins the game.
Length: 10-12 min
Variation: In this variation the point is not played out. The server scores a point if his serve is not returned. The receiver scores a point if he can return the serve.

9.

Name: Attack the Net Player
Focus: Serve and return
Skill level: Intermediate, advanced
Setup: One player starts in the returning position on side B on the deuce side. The other player starts at the net on the ad side on side A. The instructor starts at the deuce side doubles serving position on side A.
Description: The instructor serves a second serve to the player on side B who has to hit the ball down the line. The net player has to volley the ball crosscourt half-court only. If the receiver wins the point with the return, he scores a point. If the net player can hit a successful volley crosscourt, he scores a point. After 15 points the roles are reversed. The drill is then repeated from the ad side.
Length: 20-25 min
Variation: For more advanced players the instructor can hit first and second serves.

10.

Name: Avoid the Net Player
Focus: Serve and return
Skill level: Intermediate, advanced
Setup: One player starts in the returning position on side B on the deuce side. The other player starts at the deuce side doubles serving position on side A.
The instructor starts at the net on the ad side on side A.
Description: The serving player on side A hits only first serves. The receiving player scores

a point if he can return the ball around the instructor. The return can be a lob or a passing shot. If the instructor hits the ball back, the serving player gets a point. The instructor is not allowed to step outside of the service boxes. After 10 serves the drill is repeated from the ad side. The players then switch roles. The player with the most points wins the game.

Length: 25-30 min

Variation: The players and the instructor can play out the point after the serve. If the instructor wins the point, the server gets two points.

VI. *Footwork*

1.

Name: Double Side to Side Drill

Focus: Footwork

Skill level: Beginner, intermediate, advanced

Setup: One player is at the baseline and the other at the T on side B. The instructor feeds from the T on side A.

Description: The instructor feeds balls side to side alternating between the two players. He hits the balls in this order: forehand baseline player, backhand service line player, backhand baseline player, forehand service line player. Since the players are always hitting balls on opposite sides, the baseline player will not hit the service line player in the back. The drill ends after a predetermined time.

Length: 5-6 min

Variation: The service line player can be closer to the net to hit volleys. The baseline player has to be a little more careful not to hit the net player in the back.

2.

Name: Volley Overhead Drill

Focus: Footwork

Skill level: Beginner, intermediate, advanced

Setup: Both players are at the net on side B with one on the deuce side and one on the ad side. The instructor feeds from the service line on side A.

Description: The instructor feeds a volley to each player. The players then immediately back up for an overhead. The cycle continues with a volley and an overhead. The players are not allowed to let the balls bounce. The drill ends after a predetermined time.

Length: 5-6 min

Variation: The players can hit the volleys and overheads either crosscourt or down the line.

3.

Name: Circle Around
Focus: Footwork
Skill level: Beginner, intermediate, advanced
Setup: Both players start at the baseline on the ad side on side B in a single line. The instructor feeds from the T on side A.
Description: The players hit three balls each. The first player in line runs across for the ground stroke on the deuce side, then runs forward for an approach shot also on the deuce side, and finally he hits a volley from the ad side. The instructor immediately feeds the next ball to the second player deep on the deuce side. The drill ends after a predetermined time.
Length: 5-6 min
Variation: The instructor can add a lob as a fourth shot after the volley. The player has to let it bounce and return it.

4.

Name: Short and Deep
Focus: Footwork
Skill level: Intermediate, advanced
Setup: Both players start at the baseline on opposite sides. The instructor feeds from the net post.
Description: The instructor feeds the ball to a random side. The players work together as a team. Each player has to hit a short ball and a deep ball one after another. The short ball has to bounce in one of the service boxes. The deep ball has to bounce behind the service line. The players have to let every ball bounce. If a player misses a ball, the point restarts. One round consists of four shots altogether: short to short and deep to deep. The drill ends when two perfect rounds in a row are completed.
Length: 8-10 min
Variation: The drill can also be played competitively. The rules are the same, but the players score points. The game ends after a player reaches 15 points.

5.

Name: Short and Deep Volleys
Focus: Footwork
Skill level: Intermediate, advanced
Setup: One player starts at the baseline on side B. The other player starts at the net on side A. The instructor feeds from side A.
Description: The players work together as a team. The volley player has to hit one ball short and one ball deep. The short ball has to bounce in one of the service boxes. The deep ball has to bounce behind the service line. The baseline player has to let every ball bounce.

The net player has to hit every ball with a volley. The drill ends after the players reach 20 shots in a row altogether. The roles are then reversed.

Length: 15-20 min

Variation: The drill can also be played for predetermined time. The recommended time is 10 min. for each round.

6.

Name: Four Corners Drill

Focus: Footwork

Skill level: Intermediate, advanced

Setup: One player starts at the baseline on side B. The other player starts at the net on side A. The instructor feeds from side A.

Description: The players work together as a team. The court is divided into four quadrants. These are the two service boxes and the two halves of no man's land. The net player has to hit four balls in order: deep ball to the deuce side, short ball to the ad side, the ball to the ad side, short ball to the deuce side. The baseline player has to let every ball bounce. The net player has to hit every ball with a volley. The drill ends after the players reach 20 shots in a row altogether. The roles are then reversed.

Length: 15-20 min

Variation: The drill can also be played for predetermined time. The recommended time is 10 min. for each round.

7.

Name: Drop Shot Lob Drill

Focus: Footwork

Skill level: Intermediate, advanced

Setup: Both players start at the baseline on opposite sides. The instructor feeds from side A.

Description: The instructor feeds the ball to the deuce side on side B. The player on side B has to hit one ball short and one ball deep. The player on side A can only hit the ball back to the deuce side half-court only. He can hit the ball deep or short. Both players have to let every ball bounce. The first player to 10 points is the winner. The roles are then reversed. The drill can also be played from the ad side.

Length: 15-20 min

Variation: Players can also work together in this drill to reach 20 shots in a row.

8.

Name: Carousel Drill

Focus: Footwork

Skill level: Intermediate, advanced

Setup: Both players start at the net on side B. The instructor feeds from the T on side A.

Description: The instructor feeds a lob over the player on the ad side who lets it go. The player from the deuce side lets it bounce and returns it while the player from the ad side takes his place at the net. The player on the ad side now comes forward and hits a volley. The round is then repeated again and again. After a predetermined time, the instructor can feed the two balls to the deuce side.

Length: 10-12 min

Variation: More advanced players can hit the lob with a volley.

9.

Name: Mini Tennis Running

Focus: Footwork

Skill level: Intermediate, advanced

Setup: Both players start at the T on opposite sides. The instructor feeds from the net post.

Description: The instructor feeds the ball in to a random side. The players can only hit the ball into the service boxes. One player can only hit crosscourt and the other can only hit down the line. Volleys are not allowed. After the score reaches 10 points, the roles are reversed. The game ends when the score reaches 21 points.

Length: 8-10 min

Variation: The players can also work together as a team to accomplish 20 good shots in a row.

10.

Name: Side to Side Passing Shots

Focus: Footwork

Skill level: Intermediate, advanced

Setup: One player starts at the baseline on side B. The other player starts at the net on side A. The instructor feeds from behind the net player.

Description: The instructor feeds a forehand and a backhand to the baseline player. He has to hit every ball crosscourt half-court only. The net player has to return every ball crosscourt half-court only. The instructor and the baseline player work together as a team. The game ends when the baseline player can hit a passing shot that the net player can not touch. The roles are then reversed.

Length: 8-10 min

Variation: The baseline player can also hit passing shots down the line.

Three Player Lessons

This section includes, as the title indicates, three player lessons with instructor. Many times this happens when a fourth player doesn't show up for a scheduled lesson. The instructor often has to improvise and come up with a new game plan. In this case, players are usually flexible and understanding because they understand the instructor has to alter his lesson plan. Many players, especially advanced players, don't prefer this setup. However, it is a great format the practice doubles, footwork, and change of direction drills. It also allows instructor to participate in drills as a fourth player. A great feature of three player lessons is that it allows practicing singles or doubles equally.

I. *Warm-up*

1.

Name: Ground Stroke Warm-up Triangle
Focus: Warm-up
Skill level: Intermediate, advanced
Setup: Two players are at the baseline on side B, one on the deuce side and one on the ad side. The third player is at the baseline on the deuce side on side A. The instructor feeds from the ad side on side A.
Description: The players on side B can only hit the ball to the deuce side half-court only. Doubles alleys are in. The player by himself has to alternate a crosscourt and a down the line. All three players are working together as a team. The goal is to reach 30 shots in a row. The players then rotate around clockwise. After a full rotation, the drill is repeated to the ad side.
Length: 15-20 min
Variation: The players can practice singles and not count the doubles alleys.

2.

Name: Volley Warm-up Triangle
Focus: Warm-up
Skill level: Intermediate, advanced
Setup: Two players are on the service line, one side each on side B. The instructor and the third player are also on the service line, one side each on side A.
Description: The players are only allowed to volley, so they have to keep the ball in the air. The players on side B are only allowed to hit crosscourt while the player and the instructor

on side A can only hit down the line. They are working together as a team to reach 40 volleys in a row.

Length: 8-10 min

Variation: The instructor doesn't have to participate in the drill. He can only feed the ball in. In this situation, the player on the instructor's side alternates a crosscourt and a down the line volley.

3.

Name: Volley to Ground Strokes Warm-up

Focus: Warm-up

Skill level: Intermediate, advanced

Setup: Two players are at the net on side B, one player on each side. The instructor and the third player are at the baseline on side A, also one on each side.

Description: The players on side B are only allowed to volley. They have to hit every ball crosscourt. The instructor and the third player can only hit the ball down the line. Doubles alleys are in. The players are working together as a team to complete 40 shots in a row. Players then rotate positions in a clockwise order.

Length: 20-25 min

Variation: The baseline player can play from either the deuce or the ad side.

4.

Name: Ground Strokes to Volley Warm-up

Focus: Warm-up

Skill level: Intermediate, advanced

Setup: Two players are at the baseline on side B, one player on each side. The instructor and the third player are at the net on side A, also one on each side.

Description: The players on side B can only hit the ball crosscourt. The instructor and his partner can only hit volleys down the line. Doubles alleys are in. The players are working together as a team to complete 40 shots in a row. The players then rotate positions in a clockwise order.

Length: 20-25 min

Variation: The instructor and his partner have to hit the volleys behind the service line.

5.

Name: Overhead Warm-up

Focus: Warm-up

Skill level: Intermediate, advanced

Setup: Two players are at the net on side B, one player on each side. The instructor and the third player are at the baseline on side A, also one on each side.

Description: The instructor and his partner can only hit lobs down the line. The net players can only hit overheads crosscourt. All players are working together as a team. The goal is to reach 40 shots in a row. The players then rotate around in a clockwise order.
Length: 20-25 min
Variation: If intermediate players have trouble hitting lobs down the line, they can just hit lobs in a random order. The net players still have to alternate overheads to the deuce and the ad side.

6.

Name: One up One Back Warm-up
Focus: Warm-up
Skill level: Intermediate, advanced
Setup: Two players start in a one up one back formation on the deuce side on side B. The instructor and the third player also start in a one up one back formation on the deuce side on side A. The instructor starts as the net player.
Description: The players on side B are only allowed to hit the ball crosscourt. The instructor and his partner can only hit the ball down the line. Doubles alleys are in. The players are working together as a team. The goal is to hit 40 shots in a row. The drill is then repeated to the ad side.
Length: 20-25 min
Variation: The instructor can start as the baseline player.

7.

Name: Volley Rotation Warm-up
Focus: Warm-up
Skill level: Intermediate, advanced
Setup: The instructor starts at the net on the deuce side on side A. All three players form a single line behind the service line on the deuce side on side B.
Description: The instructor feeds a volley to the first person in line who returns it back to the instructor. The instructor hits the second volley down the line and the same player runs across and hits a second volley also back to the instructor. The player then goes to the end of the line. The instructor keeps the ball in play by volleying the ball immediately back to the first person the line. The players keep rotating around until they hit 30 balls in a row without a mistake. If the ball bounces, they have to start over. The drill is then repeated from the ad side.
Length: 15-20 min
Variation: To make the drill harder, the instructor and the players have to volley from the service line.

8.

Name: Serve and Volley Warm-up
Focus: Warm-up
Skill level: Intermediate, advanced
Setup: All players start behind the baseline on the deuce side serving position in a single line on side B. The instructor starts in the returning position on the deuce side on side A.
Description: The first player in line serves and approaches the net. The instructor hits the return straight back to the player who put the volley away. The next player repeats the serve and volley. The players switch to the ad side after each player completed five perfect rounds. The drill is then repeated.
Length: 10-15 min
Variation: The instructor can try to return a volley. If he is unable to return it, the player gets a point. The player reaches five points first is the winner.

9.

Name: Passing Shot Run across
Focus: Warm-up
Skill level: Intermediate, advanced
Setup: Two players start in a single line at the baseline on the ad side on side B. The third player starts at the net on side A. The instructor feeds the ball from behind the net player on side A.
Description: The instructor feeds a ball to the ad side and the deuce side. The first player in line hits both balls crosscourt as he runs across the baseline and goes back to the back of the line. The net player volleys both balls crosscourt. Doubles alleys are in on both sides. Players rotate after the baseline players hit 10 successful passing shots.
Length: 10-15 min
Variation: The passing shots can go to the singles court only. In this variation, the passing shots can go either crosscourt or down the line.

10.

Name: Lob Run across
Focus: Warm-up
Skill level: Intermediate, advanced
Setup: Two players start in a single line at the baseline on the ad side on side B. The third player starts at the net on side A. The instructor feeds the ball from behind the net player on side A.
Description: The instructor feeds a ball to the ad side and the deuce side. The first player in line lobs both balls crosscourt as he runs across the baseline and goes back to the back of the line. The net player can not step outside the service boxes and has to hit the overheads

crosscourt. Doubles alleys are in on both sides. Players rotate after the baseline players hit 10 successful lobs.

Length: 10-15 min

Variation: The lobs can go to the singles court only. In this variation, the lobs can either go crosscourt or down the line.

II.   *Ground strokes*

1.

Name: Change of Direction Drill

Focus: Ground strokes

Skill level: Intermediate, advanced

Setup: One player starts at the middle of baseline on side B. The other two players are also at their baseline on the deuce and ad sides on side A. The instructor feeds the ball from side A.

Description: The instructor feeds the ball to the deuce side on side B. The player on side B has to hit one shot to the deuce side and one to the ad side. The players on side A have to return every ball to the deuce side. Only half courts count on both sides. Players lose points if the miss their shot. Each side starts with 10 points. The side that reaches zero first loses. The game can be repeated from the ad side on side B.

Length: 15-20 min

Variation: Players can also keep their own score individually and only lose a point if they miss their own shot. The single player starts with 20 points since he hits twice as many balls.

2.

Name: Figure 8 Drill

Focus: Ground strokes

Skill level: Intermediate, advanced

Setup: Two players start at the baseline on side B one on each side. The third player and the instructor start on the baseline on side A one on each side also.

Description: The players on side B can only hit crosscourt half-court only. The instructor and the third player can only hit down the line half-court only. Doubles alleys are not in. Each player has to hit his outside shot. The players start with 10 points each and lose points if they miss the ball. The directions switch once a player is down to five points. The instructor does not keep his score. The last surviving player is the winner.

Length: 15-20 min

Variation: The instructor can also keep his score, but he only starts with five points.

3.

Name: Two on One Drill
Focus: Ground strokes
Skill level: Beginner, intermediate, advanced
Setup: Two players start at the baseline on side A one on each side. The third player starts at the baseline in the middle on side B. The instructor feeds from side A.
Description: The instructor feeds the ball to the single player who plays out the point against the doubles team. Players can come forward if there's a short ball. Doubles alleys are out for the singles player. The first side to reach 15 points is the winner. The players then rotate positions clockwise.
Length: 15-20 min
Variation: Doubles alleys can be in for the singles player for more running.

4.

Name: Deep Two on One Drill
Focus: Ground strokes
Skill level: Intermediate, advanced
Setup: Two players start at the baseline on side A one on each side. The third player starts at the baseline in the middle on side B. The instructor feeds from side A.
Description: The instructor feeds the ball to the single player who plays out the point against the doubles team. Both sides can only hit the ball on or behind the service line. Doubles alleys are out for the singles player. Volleys are not allowed. The first side to reach 15 points is the winner. The players then rotate positions clockwise.
Length: 15-20 min
Variation: Volleys can be allowed. Doubles alleys for the singles player can be in.

5.

Name: Two on One Passing Shot Drill
Focus: Ground strokes
Skill level: Intermediate, advanced
Setup: Two players start at the baseline on side B one on each side. The third player starts at the net in the middle on side A. The instructor feeds from side A.
Description: The instructor feeds the ball to one of the baseline players. The baseline players play as a doubles team. The point is played out against the net player. Doubles alleys are out on the single player's side. The first side to reach 15 points is the winner. After a round, players switch positions clockwise.
Length: 15-20 min
Variation: To encourage more lobs, the net player is not allowed to step outside of the service boxes.

6.

Name: Two on One Alternating Shots
Focus: Ground strokes
Skill level: Intermediate, advanced
Setup: Two players start in the middle of the baseline in single line on side B. The third player starts at the baseline in the middle on side A. The instructor feeds from side A.
Description: The instructor feeds the ball to the first player in line. The point is played out with the two players alternating each shot. Doubles alleys are out on both sides. The first team that reaches 15 points is the winner. After each round, another player becomes the single player.
Length: 15-20 min
Variation: Doubles alleys can be in for more running.

7.

Name: Alternating Shots with Instructor
Focus: Ground strokes
Skill level: Intermediate, advanced
Setup: Two players start in the middle of the baseline in single line on side B. The third player and the instructor start in the middle at the baseline in single line on side A.
Description: The instructor feeds the ball in and the point is played out. On both sides players alternate shots. Doubles alleys are out. The side that reaches 15 points first is the winner.
Length: 10-15 min
Variation: If the instructor is too strong, special rules can be adapted. Any time a side wins the point, they score 2 points. If the instructor wins the point, his team only gets one point.

8.

Name: Half-Court Alternating Shots
Focus: Ground strokes
Skill level: Intermediate, advanced
Setup: Two players start at the baseline on the deuce side in single line on side B. The third player starts in the same position on side A. The instructor feeds the ball from side A.
Description: The instructor feeds the ball in to the deuce side. The point is played out crosscourt with doubles alleys in. The two players on side B alternate shots. Only the single player is allowed to hit volleys. A round ends after a side has reached 10 points at which point another player becomes the single player. The drill is then repeated from the ad side.
Length: 20-25 min
Variation: Volleys can be allowed for the doubles team.

9.

Name: Alleys Triangle
Focus: Ground strokes
Skill level: Intermediate, advanced
Setup: Two players start at the baseline on side A one on each side. The third player starts at the baseline on the deuce side on side B. The instructor feeds from side A.
Description: The instructor feeds the ball to the deuce side to the single player. The single player has to hit one ball crosscourt and one ball down the line. The players on side A have to hit every ball back to the single player's side. Each side only scores points if they hit the ball inside the doubles alley. Volleys are not allowed. The first side to get to 10 points is the winner. Players rotate positions clockwise after every round. The drill is then repeated from the ad side.
Length: 25-30 min
Variation: Down the line shots that go into the alley can be worth two points if they go past the service line. The crosscourt shots can be worth two points if they bounce before the service line.

10.

Name: Baseline Battle for Three
Focus: Ground strokes
Skill level: Beginner, intermediate, advanced
Setup: Two players start in the middle of the baseline in single line on side B. The third player starts at the baseline in the middle on side A. The instructor feeds from side A.
Description: The instructor feeds the ball to the first player in line on side B who plays out the point against the single player. Doubles alleys are out. If the first player on side B wins the point, he stays in and plays another one. If he loses the point, he switches with his partner. Players are not allowed to play more than three points in a row. The side that reaches 15 points first is the winner.
Length: 10-15 min
Variation: Hitting a winner can be worth two points.

III.   *Net approach*

1.

Name: One on Two Attack
Focus: Net approach
Skill level: Intermediate, advanced
Setup: Two players start at the baseline on side A one on each side. The third player starts

at the baseline in the middle on side B. The instructor feeds from side A.

Description: The instructor feeds a short ball to the singles player who approaches the net. He plays out the point against the two players who play together as a doubles team. Doubles alleys are out for the single player. The first side to reach 15 points is the winner. After each round, players rotate positions.

Length: 15-20 min

Variation: Hitting winners can be worth two points.

2.

Name: Two on One Attack

Focus: Net approach

Skill level: Intermediate, advanced

Setup: Two players start at the baseline on side B one on each side. The third player starts at the baseline in the middle on side A. The instructor feeds from side A.

Description: The instructor feeds a short ball to a random place to the two players on side B. The players approach the net and play out the point as a doubles team. Doubles alleys are out for the single player. The first side to reach 15 points is the winner. After each round, players rotate positions.

Length: 15-20 min

Variation: Hitting winners can be worth two points.

3.

Name: Doubles Approach

Focus: Net approach

Skill level: Intermediate, advanced

Setup: Two players are in one up one back formation on side B on the deuce side. The third player and the instructor are also in one on one back formation on the deuce side on side A. The instructor feeds the ball from the net.

Description: The instructor feeds a short ball to the deuce side and the baseline player approaches the net. The point is played out on the doubles court. After a side reaches 15 points, players rotate positions clockwise. The drill is then repeated from the ad side.

Length: 20-25 min

Variation: If the instructor's team wins the point with a volley, they score 2 points.

4.

Name: Full Approach Drill

Focus: Net approach

Skill level: Intermediate, advanced

Setup: Two players start at the baseline on side B one on each side. The third player and the instructor start on the baseline on side A one on each side also.

Description: The instructor feeds a short ball to a random place. The players on side B approach the net and play out the point on the doubles court. After a side reaches 15 points, players rotate positions clockwise.

Length: 20-25 min

Variation: If the instructor's team wins the point with a volley, they score 2 points.

5.

Name: Approach Rotation

Focus: Net approach

Skill level: Intermediate, advanced

Setup: Two players start in one up one back formation on the deuce side on side B. The third player starts behind the baseline player also on side B. The instructor starts at the baseline on the deuce side on side A.

Description: The instructor feeds a short ball to the baseline player who approaches the net. The approach shot has to go back to the instructor's side. Any volleys afterwards can be hit anywhere on the court. Doubles alleys are in. After each point, players rotate positions in counterclockwise order. The baseline person becomes the net player, the net player goes behind the baseline player, and the player who was out becomes the baseline player. After the players score 20 points, the drill is repeated from the ad side.

Length: 20-25 min

Variation: The rules can be changed where the players are only allowed to hit the balls back on the instructor side. The point is played out the same way.

6.

Name: Swinging Volley Approach

Focus: Net approach

Skill level: Intermediate, advanced

Setup: Two players start at the baseline on side B one on each side. The third player and the instructor start on the baseline on side A one on each side also.

Description: The instructor feeds a deep high ball to the players on side B. One of the players takes the ball in the air with the swinging volley, and the team approaches the net. The point is played out on the doubles court. After a side reaches 15 points, positions are rotated clockwise.

Length: 20-25 min

Variation: If the attacking team hits a winner, they score 2 points.

7.

Name: Crosscourt Approach
Focus: Net approach
Skill level: Intermediate, advanced
Setup: Two players start at the baseline on the deuce side in single line on side B. The third player starts in the same position on side A. The instructor feeds the ball from side A.
Description: The instructor feeds a short ball to the deuce side to the first player in line. He approaches the net and the point is played out crosscourt with doubles alleys in. After the point is over, the attacking player goes to the end of the line. The point is repeated with the next player in line. After a side reaches 10 points, a different player becomes the single player. The drill is then repeated from the ad side.
Length: 20-25 min
Variation: If the single player wins the point with a volley, he scores two points.

8.

Name: Singles approach
Focus: Net approach
Skill level: Intermediate, advanced
Setup: Two players start at the baseline in the middle in single line on side B. The third player starts in the middle of the baseline on side A. The instructor feeds the ball from side A.
Description: The instructor feeds a short ball to a random side. The first person the line hits an approach shot down the line and plays out the point on the singles court. Only the approach shot has to go down the line; any other shot afterwards can go anywhere. After the point is over, the attacking player goes to the end of the line and the next player comes in. After a side has reached 10 points, a different player becomes the single player on side A.
Length: 20-25 min
Variation: Lower level players do not have to hit the approach shot down the line.

9.

Name: Serve and Volley Singles
Focus: Net approach
Skill level: Intermediate, advanced
Setup: One player starts in serving position on the deuce side on side B. The second player starts behind him. The third player starts in returning position on the deuce side on side A. The instructor observes from the net post.
Description: The first player on side B serves and approaches the net. The point is played out on the singles court. Players on side B rotate after each point. Once a side reaches five points, players switch to the ad side. After a side has reached 10 points, a different player becomes the receiver.

Length: 20-25 min
Variation: Lower level players can have unlimited serves to hit only first serves.

10.

Name: Serve and Volley Doubles
Focus: Net approach
Skill level: Intermediate, advanced
Setup: One player starts in doubles serving position on the deuce side on side B. The second player starts behind him. The third player starts in returning position on the deuce side on side A. The instructor observes from the net post.
Description: The first player on side B serves and approaches the net. The point is played out crosscourt with doubles alleys in. Players on side B rotate after each point. Once a side reaches five points, players switch to the ad side. After a side has reached 10 points, a different player becomes the receiver.
Length: 20-25 min
Variation: Lower level players can have unlimited serves to hit only first serves.

IV.   *Net play*

1.

Name: Volley Countdown
Focus: Net play
Skill level: Intermediate, advanced
Setup: Two players start at their service line on side B with one on each side. One player starts on the deuce side service line on side A. The instructor feeds from the ad side service line on side A.
Description: The instructor feeds the ball randomly to side B. Players on side B can only hit to the deuce court on side A. The player on side A has to hit one volley to the deuce side and one to the ad side. Only half courts count on both sides. Players lose points if the miss their shot. The team on side B starts with 10 points. The single player starts with 20 points since he hits twice as many balls. The side that reaches zero first loses. The game can be repeated from the ad side on side A.
Length: 10-12 min
Variation: Players can also keep their own score individually and only lose a point if they miss their own shot.

2.

Name: Volley Battle with Instructor
Focus: Net play
Skill level: Intermediate, advanced
Setup: Two players start at their service line on side B with one on each side. The third player and the instructor start on the service line on side A one on each side also.
Description: Both sides play as a team. After the instructor feeds the ball in randomly, the point is played out on the doubles court. Both sides can hit wherever they want. The drill ends when a side reaches 15 points.
Length: 8-10 min
Variation: The players and the instructor can start the point behind the service line and move forward as the point progresses.

3.

Name: Two on One Volley Drill
Focus: Net play
Skill level: Intermediate, advanced
Setup: Two players start in the net position on side A with one on each side. The third player starts on the baseline in the middle on side B. The instructor feeds the ball from side A.
Description: The instructor feeds the ball in to the single player who plays out the point against the doubles team at the net. Doubles alleys are out for the single player. The side that gets to 15 points first is the winner.
Length: 8-10 min
Variation: To focus more on lobs, the team at the net is not allowed to step outside the service boxes.

4.

Name: Two on One Volley Drill Half-Court
Focus: Net play
Skill level: Intermediate, advanced
Setup: Two players start in the net position on side A with one on each side. The third player starts on the deuce side baseline on side B. The instructor feeds the ball from side A.
Description: The instructor feeds the ball to the single player to the deuce side. The single player can hit the ball wherever he wants to, but the team on side A can only hit it back to the deuce side. Doubles alleys are in on both sides. The game ends when a side reaches 15 points.
Length: 8-10 min
Variation: To focus more on lobs, the team at the net is not allowed to step outside the service boxes.

5.

Name: Volley Rotation
Focus: Net play
Skill level: Intermediate, advanced
Setup: The instructor starts at the net on the deuce side on side A. Two players start at the net on side B with one on each side. The third player starts behind the player on the deuce side.
Description: The instructor feeds the ball in to a random player. The first two players play as a team against the instructor. The two player team can only hit the ball back on the instructor side. The instructor can hit the ball wherever he wants to. Doubles alleys are in on both sides. After each point, players rotate positions in counterclockwise order. After a side reaches 15 points, the round is repeated from the ad side.
Length: 10-15 min
Variation: The team can stay in for another point if they win the point against the instructor.

6.

Name: Volley Ping-Pong
Focus: Net play
Skill level: Intermediate, advanced
Setup: Two players line up single line behind the service line on the deuce side on side B. The third player and the instructor also line up in a single line behind the service line on the ad side on side A.
Description: The point is played out half-court down the line. Doubles alleys are in. The players on both sides have to alternate shots within the point. Hitting a winner is worth two points. The first side to reach 15 points is the winner. The drill is then repeated crosscourt on both sides.
Length: 15-25 min
Variation: The instructor can not score 2 points for winners.

7.

Name: Reflex Drill
Focus: Net play
Skill level: Intermediate, advanced
Setup: Two players start at the net on side A with one on each side. The third player starts at the baseline in the middle on side B. The instructor feeds the ball from behind the players at the net on side A.
Description: The instructor feeds a slow high ball to the service line to a random place. The single player hits passing shots as hard as he can. The single player gets a point every time he makes a successful passing shot. The net team gets a point every time they return a

ball. The side that gets to 20 points first is the winner. The players rotate positions clockwise after each round.

Length: 15-20 min

Variation: The instructor feeds the ball according to the single player's ability. He feeds deeper balls for more advanced players and shorter balls for lower level players.

8.

Name: Overhead Attack

Focus: Net play

Skill level: Intermediate, advanced

Setup: Two players start at the net on side B with one on each side. The instructor and the third player start at the baseline on side A with one on each side.

Description: The instructor is only allowed to hit lobs during a point. His partner can hit any type of shots. Both sides play together as a doubles teams. The first side that reaches 15 points is the winner. Players then rotate positions clockwise.

Length: 15-20 min

Variation: The team at the net is not allowed to step outside the service boxes.

9.

Name: Overhead Defense

Focus: Net play

Skill level: Intermediate, advanced

Setup: Two players start at the service line on side B with one on each side. The third player starts on the deuce side service line on side A. The instructor feeds the ball from the ad side service line on side A.

Description: The instructor feeds a lob to a random player. The players on side B play as a doubles team and start the point with an overhead. They can only hit the ball to the deuce side back to the single player. The single player can hit any type of shots anywhere on the court. He has to defend himself against the first overhead. Doubles alleys are in on both sides. After a side reaches 10 points, players rotate positions in a clockwise order. The drill is then repeated from the ad side.

Length: 25-30 min

Variation: The instructor can feed deeper lobs for more advanced players and shorter ones for lower level players.

10.

Name: Poaching Drill

Focus: Net play

Skill level: Intermediate, advanced

Setup: Two players start on side B in one up one back formation on the deuce side. The third player and the instructor start on side A also in one up one back formation on the deuce side. The instructor plays from the baseline position.

Description: After the instructor feeds the ball in, the point is played out on the doubles court. The instructor and the baseline player on the other side have to let every ball bounce. The two opposing net players are the only ones that can score points with volleys. If the instructor or the other baseline player wins the point, the score remains the same. If one of the net players wins the point, his team gets a point. The first team to get to 10 points is the winner. The drill is then repeated from the ad side.

Length: 20-25 min

Variation: In this variation, the instructor and the other baseline player can score points. The two net players score 2 points if they win the point. The game is played to 21 points this way.

V.   *Serve and return*

1.

Name: Doubles Return

Focus: Serve and return

Skill level: Intermediate, advanced

Setup: Two players are on side B in one up one back formation on the deuce side. The player at the baseline is in serving position. The third player is in returning position on side A on the deuce side. The instructor observes from the net post.

Description: The baseline player on side B only hits first serves to the deuce side. If the receiver can return the ball without the net player hitting it back, he scores a point. If the net player can volley the return in, his team scores a point. The point is only played out until the volley. Doubles alleys are in on the server's side. The first side to get to 15 points is the winner. The players rotate positions clockwise afterwards. The drill is then repeated from the ad side.

Length: 20-25 min

Variation: The serving team can score a point if the net player can only touch the return. This rule helps if the serving team has trouble scoring points.

2.

Name: Team Serving

Focus: Serve and return

Skill level: Beginner, intermediate, advanced

Setup: All three players line up at the baseline on side A in a single line. The instructor can observe from behind or from the returning position on side B on the deuce side.

Description: All three players are working together as a team. The players hit serves in a row. The goal is to hit 10 good serves in a row. The serve has to pass the baseline or the doubles sidelines on the second bounce. The instructor can judge serves from side B. If a player misses, the team starts over the count. After a successful round, the team repeats the drill from the ad side.
Length: 10-15 min
Variation: Beginner players can disregard the second bounce rule.

3.

Name: Ruler of the Court with Serves
Focus: Serve and return
Skill level: Beginner, intermediate, advanced
Setup: One player starts in returning position on the deuce side on side B. The instructor can decide the starting player by asking a trivia question. The other two players line up in single line behind the baseline on the deuce side on side A.
Description: Players can only score points from the receiving side (on side B). The players on side A are the servers. The servers need to beat the receiver both on the deuce and the ad side to become receivers. If a server loses the point, he goes out and the next server takes his spot. If he wins the point, he stays in and plays the other point. The receiver scores a point every time he wins a rally. The first player who wins 15 points is the winner.
Length: 15-20 min
Variation: Servers become receivers immediately by hitting the winner.

4.

Name: Pressure Serves
Focus: Serve and return
Skill level: Beginner, intermediate, advanced
Setup: Two players start at the baseline on side A in serving position with one on each side. The third player starts behind the player on the deuce side. The instructor observes from behind.
Description: Players start with two lives each. They rotate hitting serves to the deuce side and the ad side. One player is always waiting. Every time a player misses a serve, he loses a life. Serves have to go past the baseline or the doubles sideline on the second bounce. The last surviving player is the winner. The drill can be repeated from the ad side.
Length: 10-15 min
Variation: Beginners can ignore the second bounce rule.

5.

Name: One-out Rotation Drill
Focus: Serve and return
Skill level: Beginner, intermediate, advanced
Setup: One player is in a serving position on the deuce side on side A. The second player is in returning position on the deuce side on side B. The third player is waiting at the net post with the instructor. The player waiting first should be the strongest player.
Description: The first two players play out the point starting with a serve. The winner stays in, and the loser switches with the waiting player. The player coming in is always the serving player. Points are always played out alternating the deuce and the ad side. Every time a player wins a rally, he scores a point. The first player to 15 points is the winner.
Length: 10-15 min
Variation: The winning player can be the server every time.

6.

Name: Baseline Battle with Serve
Focus: Serve and return
Skill level: Intermediate, advanced
Setup: The first player starts on side B in serving position on the deuce side. The second player is waiting behind him. The third player starts in returning position on the deuce side on side A. The instructor observes from the net post.
Description: The players on side B play as a team. The first player on the team plays a point. He stays in if he wins and switches with his partner if he loses. The side that wins the point serves the next point. Points always alternate from the deuce side to the ad side and back. The first side to reach 15 points is the winner.
Length: 10-15 min
Variation: The side that hits the winner scores two points.

7.

Name: Return Contest
Focus: Serve and return
Skill level: Intermediate, advanced
Setup: Two players start on side B in returning position with one on each side. The third player starts on side A in serving position on the deuce side. The instructor observes from the net post.
Description: The player on side A hits one serve to the deuce side and one serve to the ad side. If he misses, he can hit a second serve. If his serve is not returned, he scores a point. If the receiver makes the return, the receiver scores a point. The first player to 10 points is the winner. Players rotate positions clockwise after each round.

Length: 15-20 min
Variation: If the server has trouble scoring points, he can hit serves to each side until he makes one.

8.

Name: Pro Returns
Focus: Serve and return
Skill level: Intermediate, advanced
Setup: One player starts in returning position on the deuce side on side B. The two other players line up behind him in a single line. The instructor starts in serving position on the deuce side on side A.
Description: The instructor hits one serve to each player. Against more advanced players, he can hit a second serve if he misses. Each player has one chance to make return. The players score 1 point for each successful return. The players keep score together as a team. The instructor scores one point for every serve that is not returned. The side that scores 10 points first is the winner. The drill can be repeated from the ad side.
Length: 12-15 min
Variation: Players can keep score individually. The instructor does not keep his score in this variation.

9.

Name: Pro Returns Doubles
Focus: Serve and return
Skill level: Intermediate, advanced
Setup: Two players start on side B in one up one back formation on the deuce side. The third player and the instructor also start in one up one back formation on the deuce side on side A. The instructor starts in serving position.
Description: The players keep their score individually. The instructor serves the ball in and the point is played out. The instructor serves five points. Players add to their individual score every time they win a point either with another player or with the instructor. After the five points, players switch positions in a clockwise order. After all players have returned, the drill continues to the ad side. The player with the most points at the end wins the game.
Length: 20-25 min
Variation: Players can only keep their score when they are with the instructor.

10.

Name: Second Serve Return Practice
Focus: Serve and return
Skill level: Intermediate, advanced

Setup: One player starts in serving position on the deuce side on side A. The second player starts behind him waiting. The third player starts in returning position on the deuce side on side B. The instructor observes from the net post.

Description: The players on side A are the servers and play out one point each. They have only one serve in each point. Players on both sides score 1 point if they win a rally. The receiver has a chance to score 2 points if his return wins him the point. The server has a chance to score 2 points if the return is missed. Players switch between the ad and the deuce side after each two points. The first side to win 15 points is the winner. After each round, a different player becomes the receiver.

Length: 20-25 min

Variation: Missing the serve can also give the receiver two points.

VI.   *Footwork*

1.

Name: Run across Grounds Strokes

Focus: Footwork

Skill level: Beginner, intermediate, advanced

Setup: All three players start behind the baseline on the ad side on side B. The instructor feeds from the T on side A.

Description: The instructor feeds one ball to the ad side and one ball to the deuce side. The first player in line hits both shots with a forehand (or backhand if he's left-handed) and goes to the end of the line. Both shots need to go crosscourt. The instructor feeds the two balls as fast as possible to keep the line moving. The drill is reversed after 5 min.

Length: 10 min

Variation: The first shot can be a backhand.

2.

Name: Inside out forehand drill

Focus: Footwork

Skill level: Intermediate, advanced

Setup: All players start behind the baseline in single line on side B. Right-handed players start on the deuce side and left-handed players start on the ad side. The instructor feeds from the T on side A.

Description: The instructor feeds two balls towards the players' backhand side. The first player in line has to run around both balls and hit two forehands. The first ball goes to the deuce side and the second one goes to the ad side. Players go to the end of the line after each two shots.

Length: 6-8 min

Variation: The players can switch up the direction of the shots.

3.

Name: Zigzag Drill
Focus: Footwork
Skill level: Intermediate, advanced
Setup: All players start behind the ad side baseline in single line on side B. The instructor feeds from the T on side A.
Description: The instructor feeds a deep shot to the deuce side and a short ball to the ad side. The first player in line hits both shots crosscourt. The instructor feeds the two balls as fast as possible to keep the line moving. The drill is reversed after 5 min.
Length: 10 min
Variation: For more advanced players the second shot can be a drop shot.

4.

Name: Touch the Net Overheads
Focus: Footwork
Skill level: Intermediate, advanced
Setup: All players line up single line behind the ad side service line on side B. The instructor feeds from the T on side A.
Description: The first player in line comes forward and touches the net with his racquet. The instructor immediately feeds a lob to the ad side. The same player runs forward and touches the net again this time on the deuce side. The instructor feeds him a second overhead and the player goes to then the line. The instructor feeds the balls as fast as possible to keep the line moving. The drill is reversed after 5 min.
Length: 10 min
Variation: The reverse part of the drill can be backhand overheads.

5.

Name: Split Drill
Focus: Footwork
Skill level: Intermediate, advanced
Setup: All players line up single line behind the baseline in the middle on side B. The instructor feeds from the T on side A.
Description: The instructor feeds one ball to the deuce side and one ball to the ad side. The first player in line only hits the first ball and goes to the end of the line. Since there are three participants, players will alternate forehands and backhands. The drill ends after 5 min.
Length: 5 min
Variation: The instructor can ask for crosscourt or down the line shots.

6.

Name: Short Ball Split Drill
Focus: Footwork
Skill level: Intermediate, advanced
Setup: All players line up single line behind the baseline in the middle on side B. The instructor feeds from the T on side A.
Description: The instructor feeds a short ball to the deuce side and another short ball to the ad side. The first player in line only hits the first ball and goes to the end of the line. Since there are three players, participants will alternate forehands and backhands. The drill ends after 5 min.
Length: 5 min.
Variation: The instructor can ask for crosscourt or down the line shots.

7.

Name: Volley Train
Focus: Footwork
Skill level: Intermediate, advanced
Setup: All three players line up single line at the T on side B. The instructor starts at the T on side A.
Description: The instructor feeds the ball to the first player in line who volleys the ball back to the instructor and goes to then the line. The instructor keeps the ball in play and volleys the next person the line. The players and the instructor try to keep the ball alive as long as possible. The drill ends after 5 min.
Length: 5 min
Variation: For more running, players can form two lines one on the deuce side and one on the ad side. Once they hit a volley on one side, they go to the other side. This is only recommended for more advanced players.

8.

Name: Around the World (3 players)
Focus: Footwork
Skill level: Intermediate, advanced
Setup: Two players line up single line in the middle of the baseline on side B. The third player starts in the middle of the baseline on side A. The instructor feeds the ball from side A.
Description: The three players are working together as a team. The instructor feeds the ball in the first player in line on side B. The player returns the ball and sprints around the court to the baseline on side A. Every player afterwards hits the ball one time again and runs around to the opposite baseline. The players try to keep the ball alive as long as possible. The players try to get to 20 shots in a row.

Length: 5-10 min
Variation: Hitting a volley can be worth two shots.

9.

Name: Overhead Tracking Drill
Focus: Footwork
Skill level: Intermediate, advanced
Setup: Two players start at the net on side B with one on each side. Third player starts at the net post on the ad side on side B. The instructor feeds from the T on side A.
Description: The instructor hits a lob over the ad side player who switches over to the deuce side. The player from the deuce side runs it down, returns it, and goes to the net post position. The player from the net position moves over to the ad side position. Players rotate around in this manner for 5 minutes. The drill is then reversed.
Length: 10 min
Variation: Instead of playing the drill for time, the round ends after 20 successful shots.

10.

Name: Hunting Practice
Focus: Footwork
Skill level: Intermediate, advanced
Setup: Two players line up single line in the middle of the baseline on side B. The third player starts at the net post on side A on the ad side. The instructor feeds the ball from the baseline on side A.
Description: The instructor feeds one ball to the deuce side and one ball to the ad side. As soon as the instructor starts feeding, the player at the net post starts to run around the instructor, around the other net post to the end of the line. The player hitting the ball is trying to hit the running player. If the ball touches the running player, the player hitting the ball scores one point. The running player can defend himself with his racquet, but the hitting player will score a point if the ball touches his racquet. Once a running player reaches the end of the line, the hitting player starts running around court and the next player comes in to try to hit him. The first player to score 3 hits is the winner.
Length: 10-15 min
Variation: The running player can drop his racquet when it is his turn to run.

Four Player Lessons

This section includes, again as the title indicates, lessons with four players and an instructor. This format lends itself doubles practice. It is very popular amongst seasoned league players. Every instructor has to be armed with a great number of drills in this field. This is a great way to practice different doubles formations, tactics, and net play. Most times the instructor doesn't have to participate in the drill. With four players, the instructor has to make sure that players keep moving and don't stand around doing nothing. It's usually though not a problem, and players rarely complain. Many drills have two rallies going on simultaneously one half courts. This is a great way to practice accuracy. Overall, four player lessons are a very flexible and popular setup.

I. Warm-up

1.

Name: Run across Warm-up
Focus: Warm-up
Skill level: Beginner, intermediate, advanced
Setup: All players line up single line behind the baseline on the ad side on side B. The instructor feeds the ball from the T on side A.
Description: The instructor feeds the ball to the ad side and to the deuce side. The first person in line hits both balls with a forehand (or backhand if he's left-handed) and goes to the end of the line. The second player in line then repeats the two shots. The instructor is trying to feed the ball as fast as possible. After 3 minutes, the drill is reversed the deuce side.
Length: 6 min
Variation: Two shots can be a backhand and a forehand.

2.

Name: Down the Line Warm-up
Focus: Warm-up
Skill level: Intermediate, advanced
Setup: Two players start behind the baseline on side B with one on each side. The two remaining players are in the same position on the opposite side. The instructor feeds from side A.
Description: The instructor feeds two balls simultaneously to the two players on side B. Both players start rallying down the line. The players facing each other work as a team.

Each team is trying to get to 50 shots first. Doubles alleys are in, volleys are not allowed. If a player misses, the instructor feeds the ball in immediately. The first team to get to 50 shots is the winner.

Length: 5-10 min

Variation: Players can only hit their outside shots.

3.

Name: Crosscourt Warm-up

Focus: Warm-up

Skill level: Intermediate, advanced

Setup: Two players start behind the baseline on side B with one on each side. The two remaining players are in the same position on the opposite side. The instructor feeds from side A.

Description: The instructor feeds two balls simultaneously to the two players on side B. Both players start rallying crosscourt. The players rallying crosscourt are working together as a team. Each team is trying to get to 50 shots first. Doubles alleys are in, volleys are not allowed. If a player misses, the instructor feeds the ball in immediately. The first team to get to 50 shots is the winner.

Length: 5-10 min

Variation: Doubles alleys can be out.

4.

Name: Volley warm-up

Focus: Warm-up

Skill level: Intermediate, advanced

Setup: Two players start behind the service line on side B with one on each side. The two remaining players are in the same position on the opposite side. The instructor feeds from side A.

Description: The instructor feeds two balls simultaneously to the two players on side B. Both players start volleying down the line. The players facing each other work as a team. Each team is trying to get to 50 shots first. Doubles alleys are in, but the ball can not bounce. If a player misses or the ball bounces, the instructor feeds the ball in immediately. The first team to get to 50 volleys is the winner.

Length: 5-10 min

Variation: Lower level players can let the ball bounce.

5.

Name: Figure 8 Warm-up

Focus: Warm-up

Skill level: Intermediate, advanced

Setup: Two players start behind the baseline on side B with one on each side. The two remaining players are in the same position on the opposite side. The instructor feeds from the net post.

Description: The instructor feeds the ball to a random player. The players on side B can only hit crosscourt, and the players on side A can only hit down the line. Doubles alleys are in. All four players work together as a team to get to 20 shots in a row. The drill is then repeated with the opposite direction.

Length: 5-10 min

Variation: Doubles alleys can be out.

6.

Name: Ping-Pong Warm-up

Focus: Warm-up

Skill level: Intermediate, advanced

Setup: Two players line up single line behind the baseline on side B. The other two players start at the same position on side A. The instructor feeds from the net post.

Description: The instructor feeds the ball to a random team. Players in each team have to alternate shots within the point. All four players work together as a team to get to 20 shots in a row. Doubles alleys are out.

Length: 5-10 min

Variation: In each team, one player can only hit forehands and the other one can only hit backhands.

7.

Name: Ping-Pong Volley Warm-up

Focus: Warm-up

Skill level: Intermediate, advanced

Setup: Two players line up single line behind the service line on side B. The other two players start at the same position on side A. The instructor feeds from the net post.

Description: The instructor feeds the ball to a random team. Players in each team have to alternate volleys within the point. All four players work together as a team to get to 20 volleys in a row. Doubles alleys are out, and the ball can not bounce.

Length: 5-10 min

Variation: For lower level players, the ball can bounce.

8.

Name: Mixed Ping-Pong Warm-up

Focus: Warm-up

Skill level: Intermediate, advanced

Setup: Two players start on side B with one at the baseline and the other one at the service line. The other two players start at the same position on side A. The instructor feeds from the net post.

Description: The instructor feeds the ball to one of the baseline players. Each team has to alternate shots within the point. The players at the service line can only hit volleys. The players at the baseline can only hit ground strokes. All four players are working together as a team to reach 20 shots in a row. Players switch positions afterwards and repeat the drill.

Length: 10-15 min

Variation: Each player has to alternate forehands and backhands. Volley players alternate forehand and backhand volleys.

9.

Name: Ping-Pong Overhead Warm-up

Focus: Warm-up

Skill level: Intermediate, advanced

Setup: Two players start at the net on side B in a single line. The other two players start at the baseline on side A in a single line. The instructor feeds from side A.

Description: The instructor feeds a lob to the first player in line. Players on side B alternate overheads. Players on side A alternate lobs. All four players are working together as a team to reach 20 shots in a row altogether.

Length: 5-10 min

Variation: The players on side A can play from the deuce and the ad side. The team hitting the overheads has to hit one ball to the deuce side and one ball to the ad side.

10.

Name: Serve Warm-up

Focus: Warm-up

Skill level: Intermediate, advanced

Setup: Two players start in serving position on side A with one on each side. The other two players start in returning position on side B with one on each side. The instructor observes from the net post.

Description: The server and the receiver on each side work together as a team. The players on side A alternate serves. The receivers have to return crosscourt. Doubles alleys are in. Good serve and return scores one point for the team. Once a team gets to five points, players rotate positions clockwise. The drill is then repeated.

Length: 10-15 min

Variation: More advanced players can reach to five points in a row. If a serve or and return is missed, the team has to start over.

II. _Ground strokes_

1.

Name: Half and Full Drill
Focus: Ground strokes
Skill level: Intermediate, advanced
Setup: Both teams start at their baseline on side A and B. The instructor feeds from the net post.
Description: The instructor feeds a ball to the deuce side on side A and another one immediately to the ad side on side B. Players play out the two balls one against one simultaneously crosscourt. Half court only, doubles allies are in. Once a player wins the point crosscourt, he immediately yells out the word "full", and from that point the second ball can be hit anywhere on the full court by both teams. If a team wins both points (both crosscourt and full court), it scores a point. If teams win one point each, nobody scores. First team to 10 points is the winner.
Length: 10-15 min
Variation: To speed up the game, teams can score with winning only one point. Another variation is where teams score 1 point for the crosscourt point and 2 for the full court point.

2.

Name: Protect Your Partner
Focus: Ground strokes
Skill level: Intermediate, advanced
Setup: One team starts at the net on side A. The other team starts 1 up 1 back deuce side on side B. The instructor feeds the ball from side A.
Description: The instructor feeds the ball in to the baseline player. He has to make sure his partner doesn't get hit by a hard overhead. Teams play out points until the score reaches 10 points. Then the baseline player and the net player switch on side B. Play continues until one team scores 20 points. Teams then switch sides.
Length: 15-20 min
Variation: The instructor can feed harder balls to simulate approach shots.

3.

Name: Figure 8 Ground Stroke Drill
Focus: Ground strokes
Skill level: Intermediate, advanced
Setup: Both teams start at their baseline. The instructor feeds the ball from the net post.
Description: The instructor alternates the feed between the teams. The team on side A can

only hit crosscourt; the team on side B can only hit down the line. Only half courts with alleys are in and no volleys are allowed. Both teams start with 20 points and lose points with every missed shot. Teams switch directions after score reaches 10 points. The last team standing is the winner.

Length: 10-15 min

Variation: This game can be played where each player keeps his own score. In this variation each player starts with 10 points.

4.

Name: Down the line Battle

Focus: Ground strokes

Skill level: Intermediate, advanced

Setup: Two players start behind the baseline on side B with one on each side. The two remaining players are in the same position on the opposite side. The instructor feeds from side A.

Description: The instructor feeds two balls simultaneously to the two players on side B. Both players start rallying down the line. The players facing each other play out the point. Doubles alleys are in, volleys are not allowed. If a player misses, the instructor feeds the ball in immediately. The players on each side play as a team but keep their score separately. Once any player reaches 10 points, the drill ends. The two players in each team then total their points and the team with more points is the winner.

Length: 10-12 min

Variation: The teams on each side can keep their score together as the game progresses. Every time a player scores a point for his team, he yells out the team score.

5.

Name: Crosscourt battle

Focus: Ground strokes

Skill level: Intermediate, advanced

Setup: Two players start behind the baseline on side B with one on each side. The two remaining players are in the same position on the opposite side. The instructor feeds from side A.

Description: The instructor feeds two balls simultaneously to the two players on side B. Both players start rallying crosscourt and play out the point. Doubles alleys are in, volleys are not allowed. If a player misses, the instructor feeds the ball in immediately. The players on each side play as a team but keep their score separately. Once any player reaches 10 points, the drill ends. The two players in each team then total their points and the team with more points is the winner.

Length: 10-12 min

Variation: The teams on each side can keep their score together as the game progresses.

Every time a player scores a point for his team, he yells out the team score.

6.

Name: Passing Shot Drill
Focus: Ground strokes
Skill level: Intermediate, advanced
Setup: Two players start at the baseline on side B with one on each side. The other two players start at the net on side A with one on each side. The instructor feeds from side A.
Description: The instructor feeds the ball in to a random player on side B. The two teams play out the point against each other on the doubles court. Teams switch positions after one of them reaches 10 points. The drill continues until one of the teams reaches 21 points.
Length: 10-15 min
Variation: Hitting a winner can be worth two points.

7.

Name: Lob Drill
Focus: Ground strokes
Skill level: Intermediate, advanced
Setup: Two players start at the baseline on side B with one on each side. The other two players start at the net on side A with one on each side. The instructor feeds from behind the service line on side A.
Description: The instructor feeds the ball in to a random player on side B. The two teams play out the point against each other on the doubles court. The team at the net can not step outside the service boxes. If they do, they lose the point. Teams switch positions after one of them reaches 10 points. The drill continues until one of the teams reaches 21 points.
Length: 10-15 min
Variation: Hitting a winner can be worth two points.

8.

Name: Baseline Battle
Focus: Ground strokes
Skill level: Intermediate, advanced
Setup: Two players start at the baseline on side B in a single line. The other two players start at the same position on side A. The instructor feeds the ball in from the net post.
Description: The instructor feeds the ball in to a random player. The first players in each line play out the point against each other. The winner stays in and the loser switches with his partner. Players can not play more than three points in a row. They have to switch with their partner even if they win the third point. The team that reaches 15 points is the winner.
Length: 10-15 min

Variation: Teams can score 2 points for hitting a winner.

9.

Name: Alternating Shots
Focus: Ground strokes
Skill level: Intermediate, advanced
Setup: Two players start at the baseline on side B in a single line. The other two players start at the same position on side A. The instructor feeds the ball in from the net post.
Description: The instructor feeds the ball in to a random player. In each team, players have to alternate shots. Volleys are not allowed. If a player hits the ball twice in a row, his team loses the point. The drill continues until a team reaches 15 points.
Length: 10-15 min
Variation: Teams can score 2 points for hitting a winner.

10.

Name: Deep Shot Drill
Focus: Ground strokes
Skill level: Intermediate, advanced
Setup: Two players start at the baseline on side B in a single line. The other two players start at the same position on side A. The instructor feeds the ball in from the net post.
Description: The instructor feeds the ball in to a random player. The first players in each line play out the point against each other. Players can only hit the ball between the service line and the baseline (into no man's land). The winner stays in and the loser switches with his partner. Players can not play more than three points in a row. They have to switch with their partner even if they win the third point. The team that reaches 15 points is the winner.
Length: 10-15 min
Variation: Lower level players can hit the ball short one time during a point.

III.   *Net approach*

1.

Name: Attack and Retreat
Focus: Net approach
Skill level: Intermediate, advanced
Setup: The players are divided into two teams and start at the opposite baselines. The instructor feeds the ball from the net post.
Description: The instructor feeds the ball to one of the teams, who play out the point. The winning team gets a short ball and attacks the net. If they win the point they score a point

and stay at the net. If they lose the point, they retreat back to their baseline, and the other team gets a short ball to attack the net. Teams can only score points at the net; baseline teams do not get points even if they win the rally. The first team to get to 10 points is the winner. This is a fast paced and fun drill that players love.

Length: 5-10 min

Variation: For an even faster pace, feed the ball immediately after the point is over. Don't wait for the losing team to get back to their baseline.

2.

Name: King of the Hill

Focus: Net approach

Skill level: Intermediate, advanced

Setup: The players are divided into two teams and start at the opposite baselines. The instructor feeds the ball from the net post.

Description: The instructor randomly feeds the ball to one of the teams. Teams play out the points, but neither team can volley the first shot. After they let the first ball bounce, they can approach the net at any time. If a team wins a point with volley, they get 2 points. First team to 21 wins the game.

Length: 12-15 min

Variation: To make coming to the net more rewarding, make volleys worth 3 points.

3.

Name: Doubles Approach

Focus: Net approach

Skill level: Intermediate, advanced

Setup: Both teams are in 1 up 1 back formation on the deuce side. The instructor feeds the ball from the net post.

Description: The instructor feeds a short ball to one of the baseline players. The player hits an approach shot and plays out the point. The next point the other baseline player gets the short ball. Once the score reaches 10 points, teams switch to the ad side. First team to 20 points is the winner.

Length: 12-15 min

Variation: Make baseline players start from behind the baseline for a tougher approach shot.

4.

Name: Middle Approach

Focus: Net approach

Skill level: Intermediate, advanced

Setup: The players are divided into two teams and start at the opposite baselines. The instructor feeds the ball from side A.

Description: The instructor feeds a short ball to the middle on side B. Teammates have to communicate to decide who will hit the approach shot. Players return to the baseline after each point. After the score reaches 10 points, teams switch sides and continue until 20 points.

Length: 12-15 min

Variation: To keep the attacking team on their heels, the instructor can mix in feeds to the sides.

5.

Name: Short Attack

Focus: Net approach

Skill level: Intermediate, advanced

Setup: The players are divided into two teams and start at the opposite baselines. The instructor feeds the ball from side A.

Description: The instructor randomly feeds the ball to one of the teams. Teams play out the point but can not hit volleys until they get a short ball into a service box. First team to 15 points is the winner.

Length: 12-15 min

Variation: Winning volleys can be rewarded by 2 points. Play this variation to 21 points.

6.

Name: Down the Line Attack

Focus: Net approach

Skill level: Intermediate, advanced

Setup: Two players start behind the baseline on side B with one on each side. The two remaining players are in the same position on the opposite side. The instructor feeds from side A.

Description: The instructor feeds two short balls simultaneously to the two players on side B. Both players approach the net and play out the point down the line. Doubles alleys are in. The players on each side play as a team but keep their score separately. Once any player reaches 10 points, the teams switch positions and play to 10 more points. The two players in each team then total their points and the team with more points is the winner.

Length: 12-15 min

Variation: The instructor can feed a regular ball to the players. Winning a point with a volley is worth two points.

Name: Approach Shot Rotation
Focus: Net approach
Skill level: Intermediate, advanced
Setup: Three players start on side B. Two players start in one up one back position on the deuce side. The third player starts behind the baseline player. The fourth player starts at the baseline on the deuce side on side A. The instructor starts from the service line on the ad side on side A.
Description: The instructor feeds a short ball down the line to the baseline player. The player approaches the net and plays out the point against the instructor and his partner. After the point is over, players rotate positions counterclockwise. The players on side B keep their points individually. Once a player reaches 3 points, he becomes the instructor's partner. Every time a player wins the point with the instructor, he scores a championship point. The first player to reach 15 championship points is the winner. The drill is then repeated to the ad side.
Length: 20-25 min
Variation: The instructor can start the point from the baseline on the ad side on side A.

Name: Approach – Volley – Overhead Drill
Focus: Net approach
Skill level: Intermediate, advanced
Setup: Two players start at the baseline on side B with one on each side. The other two players start at the same position on side A. The instructor feeds the ball from the net post.
Description: The instructor feeds a short ball to a random player. The team approaches the net and the point is played out. If the attacking team wins the point, the instructor feeds the team a volley. If they win the second point again, the instructor feeds them a lob. Any time the defending team wins the point, they score 1 point. The attacking team scores one point with the approach shot point, two points with the volley point, and three points with the overhead point. Any time the attacking team loses the point, they become the defending team. The drill ends when a team reaches 21 points.
Length: 10-15 min
Variation: The instructor can feed from side A only. The team on side B is the only attacking team. He feeds a total of 10 balls. Scoring works the same way. After the 10th ball, teams switch positions. The instructor feeds 10 more balls to the second team. The team with more points is the winner.

9.

Name: Serve and Volley Crosscourt Drill

Focus: Net approach

Skill level: Intermediate, advanced

Setup: Two players start in doubles serving position on side A with one on each side. The other two players start in returning position on side B with one on each side. The instructor observes from the net post.

Description: A random player on side A serves the ball, and plays out the point crosscourt. The server has to serve and volley. Doubles alleys are in. When the point is over, the other player serves the ball and plays out the next point. The servers play one point on the deuce side and one point on the ad side. Both sides keep their score together as a team. After a side reaches 10 points, the roles are reversed.

Length: 15-20 min

Variation: The servers can have only one serve.

10.

Name: Serve and Volley Doubles Drill

Focus: Net approach

Skill level: Intermediate, advanced

Setup: Two players start in one up one back formation on the deuce side on side B. The other two players start in the same position on side A. The instructor observes from the net post.

Description: One of the baseline players serves the ball and approaches the net. This same player serves four consecutive points from the deuce side. He has to serve and volley in each point. After the four points, the baseline player from the other team becomes the server. The drill continues until each player has served four points on the deuce side and the ad side. The team with the most points wins the game.

Length: 15-20 min

Variation: Winning a point with a volley can be worth two points.

IV. *Net play*

1.

Name: Poaching Drill

Focus: Net play

Skill level: Intermediate, advanced

Setup: Teams start in 1 up 1 back position on the deuce side on both sides. The instructor feeds the ball from the net post.

Description: The net players on each side can score 2 point by hitting a winning volley. The baseline players can come to the net at any time, but they can always score 1 point. The first team to 21 points is the winner. Teams switch to the ad side once the score reaches 10 points.

Length: 12-15 min

Variation: The game can be played where the baseline players are not allowed to volley (they have to let every ball bounce). This gives net players more opportunity to poach.

2.

Name: Keep the ball in the air

Focus: Net play

Skill level: Beginner, intermediate, advanced

Setup: The two teams start at their service line. The instructor feeds the ball from the net post.

Description: The two teams are working together in this drill. Once the instructor feeds the ball, they can not let the ball bounce. Each volley is worth 1 point. Teams can try to set a new record.

Length: 5-10 min

Variation: For a greater challenge, players need to step back to their service line after each volley.

3.

Name: Overhead Start

Focus: Net play

Skill level: Beginner, intermediate, advanced

Setup: One team starts at the net on side B. The other team starts at the baseline on side A. The instructor feeds the ball from side A.

Description: The instructor feeds a lob to the net team. They start the point with an overhead and play out the point against the other team. Teams switch roles after the score reaches 10 points. The game goes on until a team reaches 20 points.

Length: 8-10 min

Variation: The instructor can mix harder and easier lobs to challenge the net team more.

4.

Name: Figure 8 Volleys

Focus: Net play

Skill level: Intermediate, advanced

Setup: Both teams start at their service line. The instructor feeds the ball from the net post.

Description: The instructor alternates the feed between the teams. The team on side A can only hit crosscourt; the team on side B can only hit down the line. Only half courts with alleys are in. Both teams start with 20 points and lose points with every missed shot. Teams switch directions after score reaches 10 points. The last team standing is the winner.

Length: 10-12 min

Variation: This game can be played where each player keeps his own score. In this variation each player starts with 10 points.

5.

Name: 1-2-3 Drill

Focus: Net play

Skill level: Beginner, intermediate

Setup: Both teams start at their baseline. The instructor feeds the ball from the net post.

Description: There are 3 starting positions in the game: baseline, service line, and net position. When teams win a point, they move up a position. When they lose the point, they move back a position. Once they win a point at the net position, they complete a cycle, get a point, and start over from the baseline. The feed always goes to the team further back. Winning 3 cycles wins the game.

Length: 8-12 min

Variation: For the third point at the net, the team receives an overhead.

6.

Name: Overhead Retreat Drill

Focus: Net play

Skill level: Beginner, intermediate

Setup: Both teams start at their service line. The instructor feeds the ball from side A.

Description: The instructor feeds an overhead to the team on side B. The other team starts backing up immediately. After the point is played out, teams return to the original position. After the score reaches 10 points, the roles are reversed. Teams play to 20 points.

Length: 8-10 min

Variation: The overhead team has to let the feeds bounce.

7.

Name: Volley King Singles

Focus: Net play

Skill level: Intermediate, advanced

Setup: One player becomes the King and starts at the T on side A (the instructor can ask a trivia question to decide who to first player will be). The rest of the players are the challengers and line up single line at the T on side B. The instructor feeds from side A.

Description: The instructor feeds a volley to the first challenger in line who plays out the point against the King. If he can beat the King three times in a row, he becomes the new King. If he loses, the next challenger in line comes in. Every time the King wins a point, he adds to his total score. The game ends when a player has 15 King points.

Length: 10-15 min

Variation: Hitting two winners in a row against the king will immediately make the challenger the new King.

8.

Name: Overhead King Singles

Focus: Net play

Skill level: Intermediate, advanced

Setup: One player becomes the King and starts at the baseline on side A (the instructor can ask a trivia question to decide who to first player will be). The rest of the players are the challengers and line up single line at the T on side B. The instructor feeds from side A.

Description: The instructor feeds a lob to the first challenger in line who plays out the point against the King. If he can beat the King three times in a row, he becomes the new King. If he loses, the next challenger in line comes in. Every time the King wins a point, he adds to his total score. The game ends when a player has 15 King points.

Length: 10-15 min

Variation: Hitting two winners in a row against the king will immediately make the challenger the new King.

9.

Name: Volley Record Doubles

Focus: Net play

Skill level: Intermediate, advanced

Setup: The players form two doubles teams. The first team starts at the net on side B. The second team starts behind them waiting. The instructor feeds the ball from the baseline on side A.

Description: The two teams compete in hitting the most balls back without a mistake. The instructor will hit passing shots and lobs. The ball is not allowed to bounce. Once a team misses, the other team comes in. The team with the most balls in a row wins the game after five rounds.

Length: 8-10 min

Variation: The players can only hit the balls to the deuce side or the ad side. This makes the drill more challenging for more advanced players.

10.

Name: Volley Record Singles
Focus: Net play
Skill level: Intermediate, advanced
Setup: The players line up at the T in a single line on side B. The instructor feeds from the baseline on side A.
Description: The first player in line comes forward. The instructor keeps feeding passing shots and lobs to him until he misses. The goal is to return as many balls as possible without a mistake. All four players have two turns to set a new record. The player with the most shots in a row wins the game.
Length: 10-12 min
Variation: The players can only hit the balls to the deuce side or the ad side. This makes the drill more challenging for more advanced players.

V.   *Serve and return*

1.

Name: Serve and Return Battle
Focus: Serve and return
Skill level: Intermediate, advanced
Setup: The players form two teams: servers and receivers. The servers start on side A in serving position with one on each side. The receivers start on side B in returning position with one on each side. The instructor observes from the net post.
Description: The servers hit the first serve and the second serve in case they miss the first one. The receivers have to return the ball crosscourt, doubles alleys are in. If the return is good, the receivers get a point. If the return is out, the servers score a point. After a side has reached 15 points, the roles are reversed.
Length: 15-20 min
Variation: Doubles alleys are out for more advanced players.

2.

Name: Return King
Focus: Serve and return
Skill level: Intermediate, advanced
Setup: One player becomes the King and starts in returning position on the deuce side on side B (the instructor can ask a trivia question to decide who to first player will be). The rest of the players are the challengers and line up behind the baseline on the deuce side on side A. The instructor observes from the net post.

Description: The first challenger in line serves the ball to the King. He has to return it cross-court, half-court only, no doubles alleys. If the King misses the return, he has to return the next ball down the line. If he misses both returns, the server becomes the new King. Challengers have two serves in each point. Hitting an ace makes the challenger immediately the King. The King scores a point every time he makes a return. The game ends when a player has 15 King points. The drill is then repeated to the ad side.
Length: 20-25 min
Variation: The challengers can only have one serve.

3.

Name: Line Serving
Focus: Serve and return
Skill level: Beginner, intermediate, advanced
Setup: All players line up single line behind the baseline on the deuce side on side A. The instructor can observe from behind the players or from side B.
Description: The first player in line comes forward, hits a serve, and goes to the end of the line. The players keep rotating in this manner. The goal is to reach 10 good serves in a row. The serve has to bounce behind the baseline or the doubles sideline on side B on the second bounce. The instructor can judge the serves from side B. The drill is then repeated from the ad side.
Length: 10-15 min
Variation: The second bounce rule does not apply for beginners.

4.

Name: Doubles Return Practice
Focus: Serve and return
Skill level: Intermediate, advanced
Setup: One player starts out as a receiver on side B on the deuce side. One player starts at the net on the ad side on side A. The remaining two players line up behind the baseline on the deuce side on side A. The instructor observes from the net post.
Description: The first player at the baseline on side A hits a first serve and a second serve in case he missed the first one. The receiver has to return the serve avoiding the net person. If the net player makes the volley, the team of three players on side A scores a point. If the receiver makes the return around the net player, the receiver scores a point. A round ends at 10 points, players rotate positions afterwards. The drill is then repeated from the ad side once every player returned.
Length: 20-25 min
Variation: The net player can score a point even if he just touches the return. This is recommended for more advanced players.

5.

Name: Hardest Serve Competition
Focus: Serve and return
Skill level: Intermediate, advanced
Setup: All players line up behind the baseline on the deuce side on side A. The instructor observes from side B.
Description: The first player in line comes forward and hits a first serve as hard as he can. The instructor places a marked ball to the point where the second bounce landed. The remaining players do the same. The game ends after each player has hit four serves. The player whose ball is the furthest wins the ground. The drill is then repeated to the ad side.
Length: 5-10 min
Variation: If available, this drill can be played with a radar gun placed at the net. The fastest serve wins the game.

6.

Name: Serve and Return Switch
Focus: Serve and return
Skill level: Intermediate, advanced
Setup: The players form two teams: servers and receivers. The servers line up behind the baseline on the deuce side on side A. The receivers line up behind the baseline on the deuce side on side B. The instructor observes from the net post.
Description: The first server hits a first serve to the first receiver in line. The server can hit a second serve if he misses the first one. The servers score a point if the return is out or in the net. The receivers score a point if the return is successful into the singles court. The player who loses a point switches with his partner in each team. When a team reaches 5 points, teams switch to the ad side. At 10 points, teams switch roles. The teams switch again to the ad side from the deuce side at 15 points. The first team to reach 21 points is the winner.
Length: 15-20 min
Variation: The receivers can only hit crosscourt or down the line.

7.

Name: Second Serve Attack
Focus: Serve and return
Skill level: Intermediate, advanced
Setup: The players form two teams. Both teams start in one up one back formation on opposite sides on the deuce side. The instructor observes from the net post.
Description: One of the baseline players becomes the server. He serves five points in a

row. In each point he has only one serve. If the receiver wins the point with his return, his team scores two points. Each player serves five times from the deuce side and five times from the ad side. The team with the most points at the end wins the game.
Length: 10-15 min
Variation: The game can be played to 21 points.

8.

Name: Ace Game
Focus: Server and return
Skill level: Intermediate, advanced
Setup: The players form two teams: servers and receivers. The receivers start on side B with one on each side. The servers start on side A with one on each side. The instructor observes from the net post.
Description: Each server hits 20 serves. Every time they hit an ace, they score a point. The servers and the receivers switch from deuce side to ad side after 10 serves. The roles are reversed after the 20 serves. The team with the most aces wins the game.
Length: 8-10 min
Variation: Aces can be worth three points and unreturned serves can be worth one point.

9.

Name: Short Point Drill Doubles
Focus: Serve and return
Skill level: Intermediate, advanced
Setup: The players form two teams. Each team starts in one up one back formation on opposite sides.
Description: One of the baseline players becomes the server. He serves five points in a row. Players can hit second serves if they miss the first one. If the serving team can win the point with the next shot after the serve or earlier, they score two points. Each player serves five times from the deuce side and five times from the ad side. The team with the most points at the end wins the game.
Length: 15-20 min
Variation: The drill can be played to 21 points.

10.

Name: Baseline Battle with Serves
Focus: Serve and return
Skill level: Intermediate, advanced
Setup: Players form two teams. Both teams line up behind the baseline on the deuce side on opposite sides. The instructor observes from the net post.

Description: The first player in a random team starts the point with a serve. If the server wins the point, his team scores two points. The player who won the point stays in, and the loser of the point switches with his partner. The winner of the previous point is the server for next point. Teams alternate deuce and ad side after each point. A player is not allowed to play more than two points in a row. The first team to reach 15 points is the winner.
Length: 10-15 min
Variation: Winning the point with the return is also worth two points.

VI. *Footwork*

1.

Name: Zigzag Drill
Focus: Footwork
Skill level: Beginner, intermediate, advanced
Setup: All players line up behind the baseline on the ad side on side B. The instructor feeds from the T on side A.
Description: The instructor feeds a deep ball to the deuce side and a short ball to the ad side. The first player in line returns both balls crosscourt and goes back to the end of the line. Players keep rotating in the same manner. The instructor feeds the ball as fast as he can to keep the line moving. After 5 minutes, the drill is repeated to the ad side.
Length: 10 min
Variation: The instructor can hit a drop shot as a short ball for more advanced players. Players can score points for returning the drop shot. The first player to 10 points is the winner.

2.

Name: Drop Shot Sprint Drill
Focus: Footwork
Skill level: Beginner, intermediate, advanced
Setup: All players start behind the baseline in the middle on side B. The instructor feeds the ball from the T on side A.
Description: The instructor feeds a drop shot to a random side. The first player in line runs it down, returns it, and goes back to the end of the line. The players keep rotating in the same manner and score points every time they return a drop shot. The instructor feeds the balls as fast as possible to keep the line moving. The first player to return 20 drop shots is the winner.
Length: 8-10 min
Variation: The players can start from either the deuce side or the ad side. In this case, the instructor feeds the drop shot to the opposite side. This is recommended for more advanced players.

3.

Name: Around the world with 4 players
Focus: Footwork
Skill level: Intermediate, advanced
Setup: Two players line up behind the baseline in the middle on side B. The other two players start in the same position on side A. The instructor feeds the ball from side A.
Description: All four players work together as a team. The instructor feeds the ball in to the first player in line on side B. The player hits the ball over and runs around the court to the end of the line on side A. Players keep rotating in the same manner. They are working together to hit 20 shots in a row.
Length: 8-10 min
Variation: More advanced players can hit the ball either crosscourt or down the line.

4.

Name: Overhead Tracking Singles
Focus: Footwork
Skill level: Intermediate, advanced
Setup: Two players start at a net post on side B. The other two players start at the other net post also on side B. The instructor feeds the ball from the T on side A.
Description: The instructor hits a lob to the deuce side. The first player in line at the ad side net post on side B runs it down and returns it. He then goes to the end of the line at the opposite net post. The instructor hits the next lob to the ad side. The first player from the deuce side net post on side B runs it down and returns it. Players rotate in the same manner. The players score 1 point for each successful return. The first player to 10 points is the winner.
Length: 5-10 min
Variation: More advanced players can try to return the ball crosscourt or down the line.

5.

Name: Overhead tracking doubles
Focus: Footwork
Skill level: Intermediate, advanced
Setup: The players form two teams. The teammates in each team start at the opposite net post on side B. The instructor feeds from the T on side A.
Description: The first team moves into the net position. The instructor feeds a lob to a random location. The team tracks it down and returns the ball. The next team immediately moves in for the next lob. The instructor feeds the lobs as fast as possible to keep the players moving. Team score points every time they return a ball. The first team to reach 20 points is the winner.
Length: 5-10 min

Variation: More advanced players can try to return the ball crosscourt or down the line.

6.

Name: Overhead Tracking Points
Focus: Footwork
Skill level: Intermediate, advanced
Setup: One player starts at the net on side A. The remaining three players start at the net post on side B. The instructor feeds the ball from side A.
Description: The instructor feeds a lob to the deuce side. The first player in line tracks the ball down and plays out the point against the net player. If he can win the rally, he becomes the new net player. If he loses the rally, the net player scores a point and the next player comes in to track down the next lob. Once a player scores 15 points at the net, the drill is repeated from the ad side.
Length: 12-15 min
Variation: In this variation, the net player does not score points. The players tracking down the lob score points if they beat the net player. After each point, the net player goes to then the line and the player who tracked down the lob becomes the new net player. First player to 10 points is the winner.

7.

Name: Volley Train
Focus: Footwork
Skill level: Intermediate, advanced
Setup: All players line up behind the T on side B. The instructor starts at the T on side A.
Description: The instructor feeds the ball to the first player in line. He returns the ball to the instructor and goes to end of the line. The instructor keeps the ball in play and hits it to the next player. The players keep rotating in the same manner. After 5 minutes, the drill ends.
Length: 5 min
Variation: The instructor and the players can try to get to 50 volleys in a row.

8.

Name: Deep Volley Drill
Focus: Footwork
Skill level: Advanced
Setup: Two players start behind the service line on side B with one on each side. The other two start in the same position on the opposite side. The instructor feeds the ball from side A.
Description: All four players work together as a team. The players are not allowed to step inside the service boxes. They are also not allowed to let the ball bounce. They have to keep the ball in the air from behind the service line for 20 shots.

Length: 10-15 min
Variation: The drill can be played as a competition. Players have to volley every ball behind the service line. Doubles alleys are in. A team wins after they reach 15 points.

9.

Name: Poach Rotation
Focus: Footwork
Skill level: Intermediate, advanced
Setup: All players line up behind the ad side service line on side B. The instructor feeds the ball from the deuce side baseline on side A.
Description: The instructor feeds two balls in quick succession to the first player in line. Both balls are crosscourt just far enough for the player to reach them. The player goes to the end of the line afterwards. Players keep rotating in the same manner. The instructor is trying to feed the balls as fast as possible to keep the line moving. After 5 minutes, the drill is repeated from the deuce side.
Length: 10 min
Variation: The instructor can place targets to the ad side service line on side A. The player with the most hits wins the game.

10.

Name: Overhead Rotation
Focus: Footwork
Skill level: Intermediate, advanced
Setup: All players line up behind the ad side service line on side B. The instructor feeds the ball from the deuce side baseline on side A.
Description: The instructor feeds two lobs in quick succession to the first player in line. The player has to touch the net with his racquet before each lob. Both lobs are crosscourt just far enough for the player to reach them. The player goes to the end of the line afterwards. The instructor is trying to feed the lobs as fast as possible to keep the line moving. After 5 minutes, the drill is repeated from the deuce side.
Length: 10 min
Variation: The instructor can place targets to the ad side service line on side A. The player with the most hits wins the game.

Clinics

Clinics include group lessons with more than four players. This is a format that is very popular and widely used to accommodate the large number of people. Tennis camps, league team practices, high school team practices are all forms of clinics. All drills in this section are played on one court. The challenge of instructors teaching clinics is to keep all participating players moving, focused, and not bored. The drills designed for this section encourage teamwork, competitive play, and working towards goals. The section contains many drills for beginner players since this is the way many young players are introduced to the game. This chapter is also very useful for high school and college coaches who have to keep their whole team moving and focused the whole time. Even though the "Multi Court Drills" section is best suited for these teams, coaches often want to keep the team together on one court to maintain or raise team morale. The quality of clinics can sometimes make or break a tennis teacher. If the drills are good, he may be able to recruit private lessons from the clinic. If the group leaves frustrated, they may never come back again. It is the knowledge of clinic drills that separate beginner instructors from great ones.

I. Warm-up

1.

Name: Assembly Line
Focus: Warm-up
Skill level: Beginner, intermediate
Setup: All players start in a single line behind the baseline on the ad side on side B. The instructor feeds the ball from the service line on side A.
Description: The instructor feeds one ball to the ad side one ball to the deuce side. Players move along the baseline as they hit the two shots. The feed can be sped up where two players can hit at the same time. Players start from the deuce side after 5 minutes.
Length: 10 min
Variation: Players have to hit to a certain direction either crosscourt or down the line.

2.

Name: Zigzag Drill
Focus: Warm-up
Skill level: Beginner, intermediate
Setup: All players start in a single line behind the baseline on the ad side on side B. The

instructor feeds the ball from the service line on side A.

Description: The instructor feeds one deep ball to the deuce side, one short ball to the ad side. Players run the two balls down in a zigzag pattern. Players start from the deuce side after 3 minutes. This is an intense warm up drill.

Length: 6 min

Variation: The second ball can be a drop shot for more advanced players.

3.

Name: Volley Assembly Line

Focus: Warm-up

Skill level: Beginner, intermediate, advanced

Setup: All players line up behind the service line on the ad side on side B. The instructor feeds the ball from the deuce side baseline on side A.

Description: The instructor feeds one ball down the line and one ball crosscourt. The first player in line runs across the court and hits both volleys. He then goes to the end of the line, and the next player comes in. Players keep rotating this way for 5 minutes. The drill is then reversed to the deuce side.

Length: 10 min

Variation: The instructor can place a target to the ad side service line. The players have to try to hit the target with both volleys.

4.

Name: Overhead Assembly Line

Focus: Warm-up

Skill level: Beginner, intermediate, advanced

Setup: All players line up behind the service line on the ad side on side B. The instructor feeds the ball from the deuce side baseline on side A.

Description: The instructor feeds a lob down the line and another crosscourt. The first player in line runs across the court and hits both overheads. He then goes to the end of the line, and the next player comes in. Players keep rotating this way for 5 minutes. The drill is then reversed to the deuce side.

Length: 10 min

Variation: The instructor can place a target to the ad side service line. The players have to try to hit the target with both overheads.

5.

Name: Four Shot Warm-up

Focus: Warm-up

Skill level: Beginner, intermediate, advanced

Setup: The players form two lines behind the baseline on side B with one on the deuce side and one on the ad side. The instructor feeds from the T on side A.

Description: The instructor feeds four balls to the first player in each line: ground stroke, approach shots, volley, and an overhead. The players then go to the end of the opposite line. Players keep rotating for 5 minutes.

Length: 5 min

Variation: Players score a point if they make all four shots. More advanced players can hit only crosscourt or down the line.

6.

Name: Ground Stroke Line

Focus: Warm-up

Skill level: Beginner, intermediate, advanced

Setup: All players start in a single line at the middle of the baseline on side B. The instructor feeds the ball from the service line on side A.

Description: The instructor feeds one ball to the deuce side one ball to the ad side. Players hit one shot then move to the end of the line. Drill ends after 5 minutes. The instructor feeds the ball as fast as possible to keep the line moving.

Length: 5 min

Variation: The instructor can feed wider shots for more range and movement.

7.

Name: Volley Line

Focus: Warm-up

Skill level: Beginner, intermediate, advanced

Setup: All players start in a single line at the middle of the service line on side B. The instructor feeds the ball from the service line on side A.

Description: The instructor feeds one volley to the deuce side, one volley to the ad side. Players hit one volley then move to the end of the line. Drill ends after 5 minutes. The instructor feeds the ball as fast as possible to keep the line moving.

Length: 5 min

Variation: Players can get a forehand and a backhand volley when it is their turn.

8.

Name: Back of the Bus

Focus: Warm-up

Skill level: Beginner

Setup: Two random players start behind the service line on side B, one on deuce side one on ad side. The rest of the players line up behind the baseline on side B. The instructor feeds the ball from the service line on side A.

Description: The instructor feeds one ball to each player. If he makes it, he stays and keeps hitting. If he misses, he goes back to the end of the line and the player on the other side scores a point. The first player in line replaces the person who missed. The first player to 10 points is the winner.

Length: 10-12 min

Variation: More advanced players can hit from the baseline.

9.

Name: Alternating Shots Warm-up

Focus: Warm-up

Skill level: Intermediate, advanced

Setup: The players form two teams. One team starts at the baseline on side B in single line. The other team starts at the same position on side A. The instructor feeds the ball from the net post.

Description: The instructor feeds the ball to a random team. Players in each team can only hit the ball one time and have to rotate around. Players alternate shots this way through the whole rally. The two teams are working together to reach 30 shots in a row.

Length: 8-10 min

Variation: More advanced players can hit only behind the service line. If the ball short, they have to start over.

10.

Name: Alternating Volleys Warm-up

Focus: Warm-up

Skill level: Intermediate, advanced

Setup: The players form two teams. One team starts at the service line on side B in single line. The other team starts at the same position on side A. The instructor feeds the ball from side A.

Description: The instructor feeds the ball to the first player. Players in each team can only hit one volley and have to rotate around. Players alternate volleys this way through the whole rally. The ball is not allowed to bounce. The two teams are working together to reach 30 volleys in a row.

Length: 8-10 min

Variation: Once side can only hit forehand volleys, and the other side can only hit backhand volleys.

II.   *Ground strokes*

1.

Name: Run-Across Drill
Focus: Ground strokes
Skill level: Intermediate, advanced
Setup: Random player starts with the instructor at the net on side A. The instructor takes ad side, his partner takes deuce side. Other players line up in a single line on the ad side behind the baseline on side B. They keep score as one single team against the instructor and his partner.
Description: The instructor feeds the ball straight to the deuce side. The first person in line runs the ball down and plays out the point with the second person in line as his partner. Players keep rotating until one side reaches 15 points.
Length: 10-15 min
Variation: The instructor can start on deuce side and feed the ball straight to the ad side. Opposing team has to line up on the deuce side.

2.

Name: Baseline Battle
Focus: Ground strokes
Skill level: Beginner, intermediate, advanced
Setup: Divide players into 2 even teams to side A and B. Each team forms a single line behind their baseline. The instructor feeds the ball from the net post.
Description: The instructor feeds the ball in, and the first players in each line play out the point against each other. The losing player goes back to the end of the line, and the next player from his team comes in. The winning player stays and plays another point. No player can play more than 3 points in a row even if they won three times. The first team to 15 points is the winner.
Length: 12-15 min
Variation: Rules can be changed where winners are worth 2 points.

3.

Name: Tricky Feed
Focus: Ground strokes
Skill level: Intermediate, advanced
Setup: Divide players into 2 even teams to side A and B. Each team forms a single line behind their baseline. The instructor observes from the net post.
Description: The first players in each line play out the point against each other. The player

on side A feeds the ball from the baseline. He can hit any kind of crazy feed, but if he misses, he loses the point. The losing player goes back to the end of the line, and the next player from his team comes in. The winning player stays and plays another point, but this time the other team feeds the ball. No player can play more than 3 points in a row even if they won three times. The first team to 15 points is the winner.

Length: 10-15 min

Variation: Rules can be changed where winners are worth 2 points.

4.

Name: One Point Tournament

Focus: Ground strokes

Skill level: Beginner, intermediate, advanced

Setup: Divide players into 2 even teams to side A and B. Each team forms a single line behind their baseline. The instructor feeds the ball from the net post.

Description: The instructor feeds the ball in, and the first players in each line play out the point against each other. The losing player is out of the game (he can start picking up balls), and the next player in line from his team comes in. The winning player goes to the end of his line, and the next player from his team comes in to play the next point. The team that has players (or player) left is the winner.

Length: 6-10 min

Variation: For a longer game, players can have more than one life lines. Once they lose them, they are out of the game.

5.

Name: One and Out Drill

Focus: Ground strokes

Skill level: Intermediate, advanced

Setup: The players divide into two teams. One team lines up behind the baseline on side B and the other one on side A. The instructor feels the ball from the net post.

Description: The instructor feeds the ball in to a random team. The first players in each line hit one ball then move to the end of their line. Once a player misses, he's out of the game. The last team to survive wins the game.

Length: 8-10 min

Variation: Players can have more than one life.

6.

Name: Road Trip

Focus: Ground strokes

Skill level: Beginner

Setup: The instructor places cones (or balls) about 2-3 feet apart along the middle service line. Players line up level with the closest ball to the net. There should be enough distance between players to swing freely. The instructor feeds the ball from the net position on side A.
Description: The instructor feeds a ball to each player one by one. Players who hit their ball in move back to the next cone. Later if they miss a shot, they move forward. The first player to make the shot from the last cone is the winner. The round can be repeated with the opposite ground stroke. This is a great game for the youngest kids.
Length: 8-10 min
Variation: The game can be made easier if any ball that goes over the net counts as good.

7.

Name: Capture the Flag
Focus: Ground strokes
Skill level: Intermediate, advanced
Setup: The players form two teams. Each team lines up behind the baseline in single line on opposite sides. The instructor places 10 balls at the net post (5 on each side) and feeds from there.
Description: The instructor feeds the ball to a random team. The first player in each team plays out the point. The losing player goes to the end of the line. The winning player stays in and plays the next point from the service line. If he wins again, he plays a third point from the net position. Once a player wins a point from the net position, he can collect a ball from the net post for his team. The players keep rotating in the same fashion. The instructor always feeds to the baseline player. The first team to collect all five balls is the winner.
Length: 10-15 min
Variation: The player who hits a winner can collect the ball immediately for his team and go to the end of the line.

8.

Name: Baseline Defense Drill
Focus: Ground strokes
Skill level: Intermediate, advanced
Setup: Two players start at the net on side A with one on each side. Two other players start at the baseline on side B with one on each side. The rest of the players line up behind the deuce side baseline player on side B. The instructor feeds from side A.
Description: The instructor feeds the ball to one of the baseline players. After the point is played out, the players on side B rotate positions counterclockwise. The ad side baseline player goes to the end of the line, the deuce side baseline player becomes the ad side player, and the next person in line becomes the deuce side baseline player. The net players stay in the same position until the end of the round. The players on side B keep their score together as a team. The round ends when a side reaches 10 points. After each round, a new

net team is chosen.
Length: 15-25 min
Variation: Hitting a winner can be worth two points.

9.

Name: Doubles Consistency Drill
Focus: Ground strokes
Skill level: Intermediate, advanced
Setup: The players form teams of two. The first team starts at the baseline on side B with one on each side. The rest of the teams start behind them. The instructor plays from the deuce side baseline on side A.
Description: The instructor starts a rally with the first team. He hits one ball to each player. The team can only hit the ball back to the instructor to the deuce side. Doubles alleys are in. The instructor counts each good shot that the team has made. Once a team misses the ball, they switch with the next team. The team with the highest number of good shots wins the round. The drill is then repeated from the ad side.
Length: 15-20 min
Variation: More advanced players can play out the point against the instructor. The team that beats the instructor three times first is the winner.

10.

Name: Singles Consistency Drill
Focus: Ground strokes
Skill level: Intermediate, advanced
Setup: The players form teams of two. The players in each team start on opposite sides. The players on each side form a single line behind the baseline. The instructor feeds the ball from the net post.
Description: The two players from the first team start rallying with each other on the singles court. They try to keep the ball in play as long as they can, and they also count the number of good shots. Once they miss the ball, they go to the end of the line and the next team comes in. The team with the highest number of good shots is the winner.
Length: 10-15 min
Variation: More advanced players can play the point on half-court.

III.   *Net approach*

1.

Name: Rush and Crush
Focus: Net approach
Skill level: Intermediate, advanced
Setup: Players divide into teams of 2. A random team starts on side A at the baseline (instructor can ask a trivia question to determine first team). The other teams line up behind each other at the baseline on side B. The instructor feeds the ball from side A.
Description: The instructor feeds a short ball to the first baseline team, who approaches the net. If they win the point, they are fed a volley. If they win this second point too, they are fed an overhead. Once they win all 3 points, they become the new defenders on side A. If the challenging baseline team loses the point, they go to the end of the line. Teams can only earn points on side A. Teams keep their points even if they lose their position at the net. First team to 15 points is the winner.
Length: 10-15 min
Variation: For faster pace, challenging teams can immediately switch to side A by hitting a winner.

2.

Name: Offense – Defense
Focus: Net approach
Skill level: Intermediate, advanced
Setup: Players divide into teams of 2. Half of the teams line up at the baseline behind each other on side A, the other half on side B. The instructor feeds the ball from the end of the net.
Description: The instructor feeds the ball in to the first two teams, who play out the point. The losing team switches out, and the next doubles team takes their place at the baseline. The winning team gets a short ball and attacks the net. If they win their point at the net, they score a point and stay as long as they keep winning. If they lose, they go out and the other team gets a short ball. The next doubles team always comes in at their baseline. Teams can only earn points when they are on the offense, defending teams don't score. The first side to 15 points wins.
Length: 8-10 min
Variation: For a shorter game, teams can earn points every time.

3.

Name: Approach Rotation
Focus: Net approach

Skill level: Intermediate, advanced

Setup: One doubles team starts in 1 up 1 back formation on the deuce side on side A. All other players start on side B with the first 2 players in 1 up 1 back formation on deuce side also. Rest of the players form a single line behind baseline player on deuce side. The instructor feeds the ball from side A.

Description: Players on side B are the attackers score points as one team. The other team plays defenders. The instructor feeds a short ball to the baseline player on side B, who attacks the net and plays out the point with her partner already at the net on the ad side. Once the point is over, the players rotate in a counter-clockwise order. The ad side net player goes out to the end of the line, and the deuce side player takes her spot at the net. The next player in line gets the short ball. The players keep rotating until side A or side B gets to 15 points.

Length: 10-12 min

Variation: After the round, 2 new players can play as defenders.

4.

Name: 3 Cycle Clinic

Focus: Net approach

Skill level: Beginner, intermediate

Setup: Players divide into 2 player teams. Half of the teams line up behind each other at the baseline on side A and the other half on side B. The instructor feeds the ball from the net post.

Description: There are 3 starting positions in the game: baseline, service line, and net position. When teams win a point, they move up a position. When they lose the point, they move back a position and get replaced by the next 2 players from their team. Once a team wins a point from the net position, they complete a cycle, get a point, and start over from the baseline. The feed always goes to the team further back. Winning 3 cycles wins the game.

Length: 8-12 min

Variation: For the third point at the net, the team receives an overhead.

5.

Name: Approach Defender

Focus: Net approach

Skill level: Beginner, intermediate, advanced

Setup: Players divide into teams of 2. A random team starts on side A at the baseline. The other teams line up behind each other at the baseline on side B. The instructor feeds the ball from side A.

Description: The instructor feeds a short ball to the first baseline team, who approaches the net. If they win the point, they score 1 point and fed a volley. If they win this second point too, they score 2 points and fed an overhead. If they win the third point, they score 3 points and go to the end of the line. If the attacking team loses any of the three rallies, they go to the end of the line immediately. First team to 15 points wins the round. The drill ends with each team played as a defender. The overall winner is the team that scored the most points is the defender.

Length: 20-25 min

Variation: The defenders can score 2 points by hitting a winner.

6.

Name: Approach Shot Line

Focus: Net approach

Skill level: Beginner, intermediate, advanced

Setup: All players start in a single line at the middle of the baseline on side B. The instructor feeds the ball from the service line on side A.

Description: The instructor feeds a short ball to the deuce side and a short ball to the ad side. Players hit one approach shot then move to the end of the line. Drill ends after 4 minutes. This drill keeps even a large group moving as long as the instructor feeds fast.

Length: 4 min

Variation: The instructor can feed drop shots for more challenge.

7.

Name: One Bounce Drill

Focus: Net approach

Skill level: Intermediate, advanced

Setup: The players divide into two teams. The teams start on opposite sides. Each team starts with two players at the baseline with one on the deuce and the ad side. The remaining players in each team line up behind the deuce side player in single line. The instructor feeds the ball from the net post.

Description: The instructor feeds the ball to a random team. The teams play out the point, but the ball can only bounce one time on their side during the rally. All players have to rush to the net to hit volleys. If the ball bounces, the team loses the point. After each point, each team rotates positions in counterclockwise order. The ad side players go to the end of the line, the deuce side players go to the ad side, and the next player in line becomes the deuce side player. The first team to reach 15 points is the winner.

Length: 10-15 min

Variation: For lower level players the ball can bounce two times.

8.

Name: Short Attack Clinic

Focus: Net approach

Skill level: Intermediate, advanced

Setup: The players divide into two teams. The teams start on opposite sides. Each team starts with two players at the baseline with one on the deuce and the ad side. The remaining players in each team line up behind the deuce side player in single line. The instructor feeds the ball from the net post.

Description: The instructor feeds the ball to a random team. The teams are not allowed to hit volleys until the opposing team hits a short ball into one of the service boxes. The team that wins the point with a volley scores two points. After each rally, each team rotates positions in counterclockwise order. The ad side players go to the end of the line, the deuce side players go to the ad side, and the next player in line becomes the deuce side player. The first team to reach 21 points is the winner.

Length: 10-15 min

Variation: Hitting a winner with a volley is worth three points.

9.

Name: Points for Bounce Drill

Focus: Net approach

Skill level: Intermediate, advanced

Setup: The players divide into two teams. The teams start on opposite sides. Each team starts with two players at the baseline with one on the deuce and the ad side. The remaining players in each team line up behind the deuce side player in single line. The instructor feeds the ball from the net post.

Description: The instructor feeds the ball to a random team. Each team has to let the ball bounce at least one time. As the teams play out the point, the instructor yells out the number of bounces on each team's side. The team that wins the rally scores the number of points equal to the number of bounces on their opponent's side. For example, if the ball bounced 2 times on side A and 1 time on side B and the team on side B wins the point, they score 2 points. After each rally, each team rotates positions in counterclockwise order. The ad side players go to the end of the line, the deuce side players go to the ad side, and the next player in line becomes the deuce side player. The first team to reach 30 points is the winner.

Length: 10-15 min

Variation: Only the feed has to bounce. The other team can take the ball out of the air immediately.

10.

Name: Alternating Approach Drill

Focus: Net approach

Skill level: Intermediate, advanced

Setup: The players divide into two teams. The teams start on opposite sides. Each team divides into two lines behind their baseline with one on the deuce side and one on the ad side. The instructor feeds the ball from the net post.

Description: The instructor feeds a short ball to a random team. The first two players on each team play out the point against each other. The team that received the short ball approaches the net. After the rally is over, the attacking two players go to the end of their line. The team that defended the previous point gets the short ball in the next rally. After the first point, teams always defend first then attack. The side that reaches 15 points first is the winner.

Length: 10-15 min

Variation: Hitting a winner can be worth two points.

IV. *Net play*

1.

Name: Volley Train

Focus: Net play

Skill level: Intermediate, advanced

Setup: All players form a single line behind the service line on side B. The instructor plays from the service line on side A.

Description: The instructor feeds the ball to the first person in line, who volleys it back to the instructor and then goes to the end of the line. The instructor volleys it back to the next person in line and so on. This is a great warm up exercise.

Length: 5-10 min

Variation: To play this drill as a game, players are out once they miss (pick up balls). The last person standing is the winner.

2.

Name: Lob Tracking Drill

Focus: Net play

Skill level: Intermediate, advanced

Setup: Players divide into teams of 2. A random team starts on side A at the net (instructor can ask a trivia question to determine first team). The other teams line up at the net post. The instructor feeds the ball from side A.

Description: As the first team enters the court from the net post, the instructor feeds a lob over their heads. The players track the ball down and play out the point against the opposing net team. If they lose, they go back to the end of the line and the next team comes in. If they win, they replace the net team on side A. Teams score points only on side A. First team to 15 points is the winner.

Length: 10-15 min

Variation: The incoming team can hit the feed in the air.

3.

Name: College Drill
Focus: Net play
Skill level: Intermediate, advanced
Setup: Players divide into teams of 2. A random team starts on side A at the net (instructor can ask a trivia question to determine first team). The other teams line up behind each other at the baseline on side B. The instructor feeds the ball from side A.
Description: The instructor feeds the ball to the first baseline team, who tries to beat the net team 3 times in a row. If the baseline team loses the point, they go to the end of the line. Once a baseline team wins 3 points in a row, they become the new net team on side A. Teams can only earn points on side A. Teams keep their points even if they lose their position at the net. First team to 15 points is the winner.
Length: 10-15 min
Variation: For faster pace, baseline teams can immediately become net players on side A by hitting a winner.

4.

Name: Volley Battle
Focus: Net play
Skill level: Intermediate, advanced
Setup: Players divide into teams of 2. A random team starts on side A at the net (instructor can ask a trivia question to determine first team). The other teams line up behind each other at the service line on side B. The instructor feeds the ball from side A.
Description: The instructor feeds the ball to the first net team, who tries to beat the net team on side A 3 times in a row. If the challenging team loses the point, they go to the end of the line. Once a team wins 3 points in a row, they become the new net team on side A. Teams can only earn points on side A. Teams keep their points even if they lose their position on side A. First team to 15 points is the winner.
Length: 10-12 min
Variation: For more frequent rotations, the challenging net team can switch to side A by hitting two winners in a row.

5.

Name: Overhead Attack
Focus: Net play
Skill level: Intermediate, advanced
Setup: Players divide into teams of 2. A random team starts on side A at the baseline (instructor can ask a trivia question to determine first team). The other teams line up behind each other at the service line on side B. The instructor feeds the ball from side A.

Description: The instructor feeds an overhead to the first net team, who tries to beat the baseline team 3 times in a row. If the net team loses the point, they go to the end of the line. Once a net team wins 3 points in a row, they become the new baseline team on side A. Teams can only earn points on side A. Teams keep their points even if they lose their position on side A. First team to 15 points is the winner.
Length: 10-15 min
Variation: For more frequent rotations, the challenging net team can switch to side A by hitting two winners in a row.

6.

Name: Run Across Volleys
Focus: Net play
Skill level: Beginner, intermediate, advanced
Setup: All players line up behind the service line at the ad side on side B. the instructor feeds the ball from the deuce side baseline on side A.
Description: The first player in line comes forward, hits a volley, moves along the net to the deuce side, hits a poaching volley, and goes to the end of the line. This cycle continues for 3 minutes then the drill is reversed to the deuce side for 3 more minutes.
Length: 6 min
Variation: The second feed can be changed to an overhead.

7.

Name: Volley Line
Focus: Net play
Skill level: Beginner, intermediate, advanced
Setup: All players start in a single line at the T on side B. The instructor feeds the ball from the baseline on side A.
Description: The instructor feeds one volley to the deuce side and one volley to the ad side. Players hit one shot then move to the end of the line. Drill ends after 4 minutes. This drill keeps even a large group moving as long as the instructor feeds fast.
Length: 4 min
Variation: The instructor can feed balls to the doubles alley for a greater challenge.

8.

Name: Overhead Line
Focus: Net play
Skill level: Beginner, intermediate, advanced
Setup: All players start in a single line at the net position on side B. The instructor feeds the ball from the baseline on side A.

Description: The instructor feeds one lob to the deuce side and one lob to the ad side. Players hit one shot then move to the end of the line. Drill ends after 4 minutes. This drill keeps even a large group moving as long as the instructor feeds fast.
Length: 4 min
Variation: The instructor can feed balls to the doubles alley for a greater challenge.

9.

Name: You Snooze, You Lose
Focus: Net play
Skill level: Beginner
Setup: All players start at the volley position along the net on side B. Make sure there is a safe distance between them. The instructor feeds the ball from the net on side A.
Description: The instructor feeds a single volley to each player in a random order. If they miss, they are out. The last player standing is the winner.
Length: 5-6 min
Variation: The players can have more than 1 life.

10.

Name: Back of the Bus (Volleys)
Focus: Net play
Skill level: Beginner
Setup: Two random players start at the net position on side B, one on deuce side one on ad side. The rest of the players line up behind the service line on side B. The instructor feeds the ball from the service line on side A.
Description: The instructor feeds a volley to each player. If the player makes it, he stays and keeps hitting. If he misses, he goes back to the end of the line and the player on the other side scores a point. The first player in line replaces the person who missed. The first player to 10 points is the winner.
Length: 10-12 min
Variation: The instructor can mix in overhead feeds.

V.   *Serve and return*

1.

Name: Serve Survival
Focus: Serve and return
Skill level: Beginner, intermediate, advanced
Setup: All players line up behind the baseline one side A. The instructor stands behind the

baseline on side B.

Description: Players hit one serve each one after another. Their goal is to get 10 serves in a row in. Once a player misses, they go back to zero. The instructor on side B checks if the serves are good.

Length: 10-15 min

Variation: The serve needs to hit behind the baseline on the second bounce. This is a variation for more advanced players.

2.

Name: Serve Competition

Focus: Serve and return

Skill level: Beginner, intermediate, advanced

Setup: The players divide into two teams. Each team lines up behind the baseline on side A with one on the deuce side and one on the ad side. The instructor observes from behind the players.

Description: The first player in each team hits one serve and goes to the end of the line. Teams score 1 point for each successful serve. The first team to reach 20 points is the winner.

Length: 10-15 min

Variation: The game can be played as a relay race. The teams try to reach 20 points as fast as possible.

3.

Name: Target Practice

Focus: Serve and return

Skill level: Beginner, intermediate

Setup: The players divide into two teams. Each team lines up behind the baseline on side A with one on the deuce side and one on the ad side. The instructor places three targets in each service box on side B and observes from behind the players.

Description: The first player in each team hits one serve and goes to the end of the line. The goal is to hit one of the targets and score a point for the team. The first team to hit all three targets is the winner.

Length: 5-15 min

Variation: Each target can be hit multiple times. The first team to score 10 points is the winner.

4.

Name: Defenders

Focus: Serve and return

Skill level: Beginner, intermediate, advanced

Setup: The players divide into two teams. Each team lines up behind the baseline on side A with one on the deuce side and one on the ad side. One player from each team starts as a receiver against the opposing team. The instructor observes from the net post.

Description: The first player on each team hits a serve at the same time. The receivers try to return the serve crosscourt. Doubles alleys are in. They keep returning the serves until they miss. Once they miss the return, they are out of the game and the next player in line becomes the next receiver. The team that survives the longest is the winner.

Length: 10-15 min

Variation: The receivers are not out of the game if they miss. They go to the end of their line and become servers. The next player in line takes their spot. The receivers score a point every time they make a return. The first team to score 15 points is the winner.

5.

Name: Point Play Defenders

Focus: Serve and return

Skill level: Intermediate, advanced

Setup: The players divide into two teams. Each team lines up behind the baseline on side A with one on the deuce side and one on the ad side. One player from each team starts as a receiver against the opposing team. The instructor observes from the net post.

Description: The first player on one of the teams serves and plays out the point crosscourt against the opposing receiver. Doubles alleys are in. If the receiver loses the point, he is out of the game and the next player in line becomes the next receiver. The teams alternate points. The team that survives the longest is the winner.

Length: 10-15 min

Variation: The receivers are not out of the game if they lose the point. They go to the end of their line and become servers. The next player in line takes their spot. The first team to score 15 points is the winner.

6.

Name: Rulers of the Court

Focus: Serve and return

Skill level: Intermediate, advanced

Setup: The players form two player teams. One team starts on side B in one up one back formation on the deuce side. A second team starts on side A in the same formation. The rest of the teams line up behind the team on side A. The instructor observes from the net post.

Description: The team on side B is the ruling team. The rest of the teams are the challengers. The challengers need to beat the rulers on the deuce and the ad side to take their spot. The rulers score points every time they win a rally. If a challenger loses a point, the next challenger takes her spot. The first team to score 15 points is the winner.

Length: 15-20 min
Variation: The challengers can become rulers immediately by hitting a winner.

7.

Name: Rulers of the Court (2 back formation)
Focus: Serve and return
Skill level: Intermediate, advanced
Setup: The players form two player teams. One team starts on side B in two back formation. A second team starts on side A in one up, one back formation. The rest of the teams line up behind the team on side A. The instructor observes from the net post.
Description: The team on side B is the ruling team. The rest of the teams are the challengers. The challengers need to beat the rulers on the deuce and the ad side to take their spot. The rulers score points every time they win a rally. If a challenger loses a point, the next challenger takes her spot. The first team to score 15 points is the winner.
Length: 10-15 min
Variation: The challengers can become rulers immediately by hitting a winner.

8.

Name: Volleyball Clinic
Focus: Serve and return
Skill level: Intermediate, advanced
Setup: The players form two teams. One team starts on side A, the other on side B. On each side, two players start in one up one back formation on the deuce side. The rest of the players on each team line up behind their baseline player in a single line. The instructor observes from the net post.
Description: One of the teams serves the ball and plays out the point against the other two players. After each point, players rotate positions counterclockwise. The players from the deuce side move to the ad side, players from the ad side move to the end of the line, and the first player in line becomes the next baseline player on the deuce side. The team that wins the point serves the next point. Only the serving team can score points. The game ends when a side reaches 10 points. The drill is then repeated from the ad side.
Length: 15-20 min
Variation: Both the serving and the receiving team can score points.

9.

Name: In and Out Clinic
Focus: Server and return
Skill level: Intermediate, advanced
Setup: Two random players start in one up, one back formation on side A on the deuce side.

Two other random players start on this information on side B. The rest of the players form two lines, one on each net post. The instructor observes from the net post.

Description: One of the baseline players starts the point with a serve. Each member in the winning team scores a point individually. The player that missed the ball goes out to the end of one of the lines at the net post. The first player from the opposite line comes in and replaces him. The player coming in to play is always the server in the next point. The players alternate deuce and ad side points. Players always keep score individually. In case of a winner, the player whose side the winner was hit on goes out. The first player to 10 points is the winner.

Length: 10-15 min

Variation: Players can form only one line at one net post to simplify the drill.

10.

Name: In and Out Team Clinic

Focus: Serve and return

Skill level: Intermediate, advanced

Setup: The players form teams of two. Two teams start on opposite sides in one up, one back formation on the deuce side. The rest of the teams line up at one of the net post. The instructor observes from the net post.

Description: One of the baseline players starts the point with a serve. The team that wins the rally, scores a point and stays in. The losing team moves to the end of the line, and the next team in line replaces them. The team coming in is always the serving team. The players alternate deuce and ad side points. The first team to reach 15 points is the winner.

Length: 10-15 min

Variation: Hitting a winner is worth two points.

VI.   *Footwork*

1.

Name: Swiss Handball

Focus: Footwork

Skill level: Beginner, intermediate, advanced

Setup: Players divide into two teams and take a position anywhere on half-court on side A. One racquet is placed in each doubles alleys at the end of the service line. The instructor starts behind the baseline on side A. The players do not have racquets.

Description: The instructor feeds a ball high in the air. The players have to pass the ball to each other. They are not allowed to run with the ball. When they receive the ball, they have to touch the ground with it before they can pass it. Players have 3 seconds to pass the ball

along. If the ball goes out of bounds, the team that knocked the ball out of bounds has to let the opposite team put it back in play. The goal is to place the ball on the opponent's tennis racquet. Once a team is successful, they score a point. The game ends when a team reaches 5 points.
Length: 10-12 min
Variation: Larger teams can play on the larger area.

2.

Name: Yo-yo
Focus: Footwork
Skill level: Beginner, intermediate, advanced
Setup: The instructor starts at the T on side A. The players line up behind the baseline on side B.
Description: The instructor hits four balls to the first player in line: drop shot to the deuce side, lob to the deuce side, drop shot to the ad side, lob to the ad side. The player goes to the end of the line afterwards, and the next player comes in.
Length: 5 min
Variation: The instructor can make this drill a game by awarding a point to the players that complete the round flawlessly.

3.

Name: Cat and Mouse
Focus: Footwork
Skill level: Beginner, intermediate, advanced
Setup: Players scatter around half-court on side A. One player is named the cat and holds a ball. The rest of the players are the mice.
Description: The cat is trying to catch all the mice by tagging them with the ball. Once a mouse is tagged, he becomes a cat also. The last mouse to survive is the winner. After around is over, another player is named the cat. If players step outside of the court, they become cats.
Length: 5-8 min
Variation: Larger groups can play the game on a larger area.

4.

Name: Lob and Catch
Focus: Ground strokes
Skill level: Beginner, intermediate, advanced
Setup: First half of the players line up at the net post on the deuce side and the second half at the other net post on the ad side. The instructor feeds from the service line on side A.

Description: The instructor alternate lobs to the deuce and ad side. The first person in line on the opposite side runs it down and returns it. After the shot, players go back to the end of the opposite line.
Length: 5 min
Variation: Advanced players can hit behind the back or "tweener" shots.

5.

Name: Side to Side Drill
Focus: Footwork
Skill level: Beginner, intermediate, advanced
Setup: The players form a single line behind the baseline in the middle on side B. The instructor feeds from the T on side A.
Description: The instructor alternates feeds to the deuce side and the ad side to the first player in line. The player has to hit every ball crosscourt. His goal is to reach 20 points. He loses a point every time he misses. After he completes a round, he moves to the end of the line and the next player in line takes his spot. The drill ends when each player has reached 20 points.
Length: 10-15 min
Variation: Beginner players can do the drill from the service line.

6.

Name: Side to Side Passing Shot Drill
Focus: Footwork
Skill level: Intermediate, advanced
Setup: The players form two teams. One team lines up behind the baseline in the middle on side B. The other team lines up behind the service line in the middle on side A. The instructor feeds from side A.
Description: The instructor alternates feeds to the deuce side and the ad side to the first player in line on side B. The player hits passing shots down the line only. The first player in line on side A tries to volley them back down the line. The instructor feeds 20 balls in quick succession. The team on side B scores a point every time the player hits a successful passing shot or the volley player misses the volley. The team on side A scores a point every time the volley player makes the volley down the line. After the 20 balls, the next two players in line come forward and repeat the round.
Length: 15-20 min
Variation: The passing shots can go crosscourt.

7.

Name: Side to Side Ground Stroke Drill
Focus: Footwork
Skill level: Intermediate, advanced
Setup: The players form two teams. One team lines up behind the baseline in the middle on side B. The other team starts in the same position on side A. The instructor feeds from side A.
Description: The instructor alternates feeds to the deuce side and the ad side to the first player in line on side B. The player hits ground strokes down the line only. The first player in line on side A tries to return them back down the line. The instructor feeds 20 balls in quick succession. The team on side B scores a point every time the player on side A misses his shot. The team on side A scores a point every time the player makes the return down the line. After the 20 balls, the next two players in line come forward and repeat the round.
Length: 15-20 min
Variation: Every shot needs to go crosscourt.

8.

Name: Side to Side Overhead Drill
Focus: Footwork
Skill level: Intermediate, advanced
Setup: The players form two teams. One team lines up behind the baseline in the middle on side A. The other team lines up behind the service line in the middle on side B. The instructor feeds from side A.
Description: The instructor alternates lobs to the deuce side and the ad side to the first player in line on side B. The player hits overheads down the line only. The first player in line on side A tries to return them back down the line. The instructor feeds 20 lobs in quick succession. The team on side B scores a point every time the player on side A misses his shot. The team on side A scores a point every time the player makes the return down the line. After the 20 balls, the next two players in line come forward and repeat the round.
Length: 15-20 min
Variation: Every shot needs to go crosscourt.

9.

Name: Mixed Passing Shot Drill
Focus: Footwork
Skill level: Beginner, intermediate, advanced
Setup: The players form two teams. One team lines up behind the baseline in the middle on side B. The other team lines up behind the service line in the middle on side A. The instructor feeds from side A.

Description: The instructor feeds random balls all over the court to the first player in line on side B. He has to let every ball bounce. The player has to hit passing shots to the first player in line on side A. The volley player on side A tries to volley them back anywhere on the court. The instructor feeds 20 balls in quick succession. The team on side B scores a point every time the player hits a successful passing shot or the volley player misses the volley. The team on side A scores a point every time the volley player makes the volley. After the 20 balls, the next two players in line come forward and repeat the round.

Length: 15-20 min

Variation: Beginner players can work together as the baseline in the volley player. Once the volley player makes 20 successful volleys, the next team comes in.

10.

Name: Deep and Short Drill

Focus: Footwork

Skill level: Beginner, intermediate, advanced

Setup: The players form two teams. One team lines up behind the baseline in the middle on side B. The other team starts in the same position on side A. The instructor feeds from side A.

Description: The instructor feeds the ball to the first player in line who starts rallying with the first person in line on the opposite side. The players on both sides have to alternate ground strokes and volleys. The players are working together to make as many good shots in a row as possible. Once a player misses, both players go to the end of their line. The drill ends when a pair of players reaches 20 shots in a row.

Length: 10-15 min

Variation: To make the drill easier for beginners, they can hit two ground strokes and one volley.

Fun Drills

This chapter is a little different. You will notice that drills have only one word in the focus category and it is fun. This is a collection of games for any size groups that come to play tennis just for fun, and instructions are not their first priority (or at least not yet). Of course, teachers will provide instructions during the course of the drills. It is important though for the instructor to keep the flow of the games moving. Many of these drills have themes that allow very young age groups role-playing. It is a great tool that helps to keep the interest and attention of these kids. This chapter though was not made only for beginners. Intermediate or even advanced players like to play some of these drills too. The instructor can implement these at the end of a more serious session.

1.

Name: Around the World
Focus: Fun
Skill level: Beginner, intermediate
Setup: Divide players to 2 even teams to side A and B. Each team forms a single line behind their baseline. The instructor feeds from side A.
Description: The instructor feeds the ball in to the first person in line on side B, who hits the ball over then runs around the court to the end of the line on side A. The first person in each line hits one ball only and runs around the same way. Once a player misses, he is out of the game (he can pick up balls). The last player standing is the winner.
Length: 10-12 min
Variation: For a longer game, players can have more than one life lines. Once they lose them, they are out of the game.

2.

Name: Wipeout
Focus: Fun
Skill level: Beginner, intermediate
Setup: Divide players to 2 even teams to side A and B. Each team forms a single line behind their baseline. The instructor feeds from the net post.
Description: The instructor feeds the ball in, and the first players in each line play out the point against each other on the singles court. The losing player goes out and to the end of the line. The winning player stays and brings in the next player in line to help him win the next point. If they win again, they can bring in a third player and so on. The team that can bring all its players into play wins the game. Any time a team loses a point, they go back to

one player.

Length: 8-15 min

Variation: If teams are not even in numbers, the team with fewer players has to win one extra point to win the game.

3.

Name: Hit to Any Court

Focus: Fun

Skill level: Beginner, intermediate

Setup: Players need to use at least 2 courts for this drill, but it is best played on 3 courts. Each player takes a side at the baseline on every court that is used. With more players, two players can be on one side and play from half court. The instructor feeds the ball from behind the courts in the middle.

Description: The instructor feeds the ball to a random side. Players can hit the ball to any court with a player on the opposite side. Once a player misses, he is out of the game (start picking up balls). If played with 3 courts, the middle court always has to have players on both sides. Once there are only two players left, they play out the last point on two courts from the opposite sides. The last player standing wins the game.

Length: 5-7 min

Variation: Players can have more than 1 life for a longer game.

4.

Name: Jabba the Hut

Focus: Fun

Skill level: Beginner, intermediate

Setup: Exactly 6 players are needed for this drill with 3 player teams on each side. One player in each team kneels down at the T on their side. The other players are at the baseline. The instructor feeds from the net post.

Description: The instructor feeds the ball to one the baseline players. The two teams play out the point against each other for 1 point each. If during the rally any of the two kneeling players hit the ball over and in, their team immediately scores 3 points even if they lose the point eventually. The first team to 21 points is the winner.

Length: 8-10 min

Variation: The players at the T can sit in a chair instead of kneeling.

5.

Name: Jail
Focus: Fun
Skill level: Beginner
Setup: All players line up behind the service line on side B in a single line. The instructor feeds the ball from the T on side A.
Description: The instructor feeds a ball to the first person in line. If he makes it, he is safe and goes back to the end of the line. If he misses, he is in "jail" and goes to side A where he tries to catch the balls that the others are hitting. Once he catches a ball in the air or after one bounce, he is out of "jail" and goes to the end of the line on side B. The person who hit the ball to him goes to jail instead. The last person standing is the winner. This is a very popular drill with many variations.
Length: 8-10 min
Variation: To make the game harder, players can hit two balls in to stay out of "jail".

6.

Name: Dragon's Lair
Focus: Fun
Skill level: Beginner
Setup: All players line up behind the service line on side B in a single line. The instructor feeds foam balls from the T on side A.
Description: The theme of this drill is that the players are held as prisoners by an evil dragon (the instructor). They can only get out by hitting a good forehand and a good backhand. Once someone gets out, he starts running to the side fence while the instructor throws balls at him (gently). If he gets hit, he is caught and returns to the end of the line. If he reaches the fence, he is safe and wins the game. This drill is best played with the youngest players. It is very popular.
Length: 5-7 min
Variation: The drill can be played until all the players get out.

7.

Name: Ping Pong Tennis
Focus: Fun
Skill level: Intermediate, advanced
Setup: Divide players to 2 even teams to side A and B. Each team forms a single line behind their baseline. The instructor feeds from the net post.
Description: The instructor feeds the ball to one of the teams. Team members need to alternate shots within the rally. If a player hits two shots in a row, his team loses the point. The first team to get to 15 points is the winner.

Length: 10-15 min
Variation: The game can be played where winners are worth 2 points.

8.

Name: Pass the Racquet
Focus: Fun
Skill level: Intermediate, advanced
Setup: Divide players to 2 even teams to side A and B. Each team forms a single line behind their baseline. Only one player starts with a racquet in each team. The instructor feeds from the net post.
Description: The instructor feeds the ball to one of the teams. Teammates need to alternate shots by passing the racquet to each other. If a player hits two shots in a row, his team loses the point. The first team to get to 15 points is the winner. The drill is best played with intermediate players.
Length: 10-15 min
Variation: The game can be played in one or both service boxes only.

9.

Name: Pick-up Drill
Focus: Fun
Skill level: Intermediate, advanced
Setup: Four players are needed for this drill. The two teams start at their service line. The instructor feeds the ball from the net post.
Description: The instructor feeds random balls not directly to the players but just behind the net. He tries to make sure his feed doesn't bounce up higher than the top of the net. Players play out the points to 11. The game has a twist though. Once a team reaches 10 points (match point), they have to back up to the baseline because the losing team gets a high overhead feed (ball has to bounce before they can hit the overhead). The losing team keeps getting high feeds until they either lose or tie the game at 10 points. If they tie, the other team gets a short low feed again, so they have to come back to the net. Teams down to match point keep getting high overhead feeds until the game ends. This is a very fast and popular drill.
Length: 5-8 min
Variation: When a team is getting high feeds, teammates have to alternate hitting the overheads.

10.

Name: Mini Tennis
Focus: Fun
Skill level: Beginner, intermediate, advanced
Setup: Four players are needed for this drill. The two teams start at their service line. The instructor feeds the ball from the net post.
Description: The instructor alternates the feed between the two sides. Players can only hit balls to the service boxes. Hard shots are not allowed. The first team to 10 points is the winner.
Length: 6-8 min
Variation: For more advanced players, the court can be extended into the doubles alleys.

11.

Name: Volleyball Tennis
Focus: Fun
Skill level: Intermediate, advanced
Setup: Four players are needed for this drill. The two teams start at their service line. The instructor feeds the ball from the net post.
Description: The instructor alternates the feed between the two sides. Only the service boxes are in. Players have to pass the ball to their partner in the air before they can return it to the opposite side. Hard shots are not allowed. The first team to 10 points is the winner.
Length: 7-9 min
Variation: For more advanced players, the court can be extended into the doubles alleys or even the whole court.

12.

Name: Hitters and Catchers
Focus: Fun
Skill level: Beginner, intermediate
Setup: Divide players to 2 even teams to side A and B. Each team forms a single line behind their baseline. The team on side B starts with no racquets; they are the catchers. The other team is the hitters. The instructor feeds the ball from side A.
Description: The instructor feeds the ball to the catchers. The first player catches the ball, throws it over, and goes to the end of the line. Catchers are not allowed to run with the ball. The first hitter tries to return it then goes to the end of his line. Players on both teams rotate in the same fashion until the end of the point. Teams then change roles at 10 points and keep adding to their score. The first team to 20 is the winner.
Length: 10-15 min
Variation: Players can play out a whole point and rotate afterwards. The winner of the point

can stay in to play an extra point.

13.

Name: Guess the Ball
Focus: Fun
Skill level: Beginner
Setup: All players start at the net on side B; the instructor feeds the ball from the service line on side A.
Description: The instructor feeds balls close to the baseline and the doubles sidelines. The players are not allowed to look at where the ball bounces and have to guess if the ball was in or out. The players who guessed wrong are out of the game. The last player standing is the game winner.
Length: 5-8 min
Variation: Players can have more than 1 life.

14.

Name: Alligator
Focus: Fun
Skill level: Beginner
Setup: All players start at the volley position along the net on side B. Make sure there is a safe distance between them. The instructor feeds the ball from the net on side A.
Description: The instructor feeds a single volley to each player. If they make it, they are safe from the alligator. If they miss, they start losing body parts to the alligator. First they have to put an arm behind their back, then they have to lift a leg, then they have to kneel down, and finally they have to sit down. Once they miss the sitting shot, they are out of the game. Last person surviving wins. Kids love this game.
Length: 8-10 min
Variation: In one variation players can get back body parts one by one if they make a good shot. In another variation players can back up a step after each good volley. Once they reach the service line (or a cone), they win the game.

15.

Name: Alligator Hunters
Focus: Fun
Skill level: Beginner
Setup: All players start at the volley position along the net on side B. Make sure there is a safe distance between them. One or more targets are setup on side A in the service boxes. The instructor feeds the ball from the net on side A.
Description: The instructor feeds a single volley to each player. Players try to hunt the alli-

gators by hitting the targets. If they hit the target, they get one point for shooting the alligator. If they miss the target, the next person will try. If they miss the volley altogether, they start losing body parts to the alligator. First they have to put an arm behind their back, then they have to lift a leg, then they have to kneel down, and finally they have to sit down. Once they miss the sitting shot, they are out of the game. Player with most kills wins the game.

Length: 8-10 min

Variation: In one variation players can get back body parts one by one if they make a good shot.

16.

Name: Figure 8 Mini Tennis

Focus: Fun

Skill level: Beginner, intermediate, advanced

Setup: Both teams start at their service line. The instructor feeds the ball from the net post.

Description: The instructor alternates the feed between the teams. The team on side A can only hit crosscourt; the team on side B can only hit down the line. Only service boxes are in (alleys can be included). Both teams start with 20 points and lose points with every missed shot. Teams switch directions after score reaches 10 points. The last team standing is the winner.

Length: 10-12 min

Variation: This game can be played where each player keeps his own score. In this variation each player starts with 10 points.

17.

Name: Scramble Drill

Focus: Fun

Skill level: Beginner

Setup: The players divide into two teams. One team spreads across side B and the other side A. The instructor feeds the ball from the net post.

Description: The instructor feeds the ball in to a random team. Before a team can return the ball to the other side, every player on the team has to touch it at least once. The number of bounces doesn't matter. Players can bounce the ball on their racket or on the ground then pass it to their teammates. Hitting the ball hard is not allowed. The first team to get to 10 points is the winner.

Length: 10-12 min

Variation: More advanced players can only touch the ball one or two times.

18.

Name: D-Day Drill
Focus: Fun
Skill level: Beginner
Setup: The instructor starts on the service line on side A. All players start on side B at the back fence holding the ball on their racket. One player who is assigned to be the medic does not have a racquet or a ball.
Description: The instructor yells go and starts feeding high balls to side B. The players' objective is to carry the ball they are holding all the way to the instructor's basket and walk back to the back fence on side B. They are not allowed to run, only walk. Also, if they get hit by a ball, they must freeze in place. The medic needs to touch frozen players to allow them to keep moving. If someone gets hit twice, they are out of the game. All players who survive win the game. The first person to return to the back fence gets a bonus point.
Length: 5 min
Variation: Lower level players only need to take the ball to the net and drop it over.

19.

Name: Robbers Drill
Focus: Fun
Skill level: Beginner, intermediate, advanced
Setup: Players form a circle of about 20 feet in diameter on one side. They place their racquets on the ground. The racquets shouldn't be closer than 6 feet to each other. Place two more balls as there are players in the middle of the circle.
Description: The objective of the game is to collect three balls and place them on the racquet. Players can get balls from the middle or from each other. Stealing somebody else's ball from their racquet is legal. Once a player has three balls on his racquet, the game ends.
Length: 1-3 min
Variation: If players have trouble collecting three balls, add more balls to the middle.

20.

Name: Ground Stroke Relay
Focus: Fun
Skill level: Beginner, intermediate
Setup: Half of the players line up behind the baseline on the deuce side, the other half on the ad side. The instructor feeds the ball from the service line on side A.
Description: The instructor alternates the feed between the two lines. The first player in each line comes forward, hits a ground stroke, and goes to the end of the line. If the player makes the shot, his team gets a point. The first team to 20 points wins the game.
Length: 5-8 min

Variation: Beginner level players can hit two shots.

21.

Name: Two Touch Tennis
Focus: Fun
Skill level: Intermediate, advanced
Setup: The players form two doubles teams. Each team starts at the baseline on opposite sides. The instructor feeds from the net post.
Description: The instructor feeds the ball to a random team. Each player has to touch the ball twice before hitting it back to the opposite side. The doubles alleys are in. The first team to get to 15 points is the winner.
Length: 10-15 min
Variation: Lower level players can play mini tennis in the service boxes with the same rules.

22.

Name: Circle of Fear
Focus: Fun
Skill level: Intermediate, advanced
Setup: The players form a circle on one half of a court. The instructor feeds the ball from the middle of the circle.
Description: The instructor feeds the ball to a random player. Players have to pass the ball to someone else without letting it bounce. The player who lets the ball bounce is out of the game. The last surviving player is the winner.
Length: 5-10 min
Variation: The circle gets bigger with each elimination.

23.

Name: Pass the Ball
Focus: Fun
Skill level: Intermediate, advanced
Setup: Players form teams of two. The instructor may pair up with a player left over.
Description: One player in each team starts at the doubles sideline. The other team member faces him from the singles sideline across the doubles alley. One player in each team has a ball on the racquet. Players try to pass or hit the ball to their teammates who then try to catch the ball only with their racquet without letting it bounce. Unsuccessful teams are out of the game. After each ball pass, team members get further away from each other. The last team to survive is the winner.**Length**: 8-10 min
Variation: Lower level players can use their hands to catch the ball.

24.

Name: Yo-yo Volleys
Focus: Fun
Skill level: Intermediate, advanced
Setup: Players form teams of two. The instructor may pair up with a player left over. Both players start at the T on opposite sides.
Description: The players start volleying back and forth to each other. As they keep the ball in the air, they move along the service line from sideline to sideline. The players can try to set a personal record of how many times they go from side to side.
Length: 5-8 min
Variation: Better players have to alternate forehand and backhand volleys.

Multi Court Drills

This section includes clinics within instructor that are played on multiple courts. Many times coaches have access to more than one court. This is the case with high school and college coaches for example. It sometimes makes sense to spread out the players to many courts to accomplish more. Some drills in this section establish a hierarchy within the courts. It allows players to prove themselves and work their way up to higher courts. It is a very effective technique. One thing is different in this chapter, and that is the lack of footwork section. Most footwork exercises require constant feeding from the instructor which can be really hard to accomplish to multiple courts. There are simply better ways to practice footwork than with multiple courts drills.

I. *Warm-up*

1.

Name: Half-Court Warm-Up (down the line)
Focus: Warm-up
Skill level: Intermediate, advanced
Setup: Players start at the baseline on each court with one on the deuce side and one on the ad side. The instructor observes from behind the courts.
Description: Players start rallying down the line with the person facing them. Doubles alleys are in. The first team to reach 50 shots wins the drill.
Length: 5-8 min
Variation: Players have to hit their outside shots. After the 50 shots are reached, players switch positions and repeat the drill.

2.

Name: Half-Court Warm-Up (crosscourt)
Focus: Warm-up
Skill level: Intermediate, advanced
Setup: Players start at the baseline on each court with one on the deuce side and one on the ad side. The instructor observes from behind the courts.
Description: Players start rallying crosscourt with the person across the court on the opposite side. Doubles alleys are in. The first team to reach 50 shots wins the drill. The players then switch positions from deuce side to ad side and repeat the drill.
Length: 5-8 min

Variation: Players have to hit their outside shots.

3.

Name: Volley and Overhead Warm-Up
Focus: Warm-up
Skill level: Intermediate, advanced
Setup: Players on side B start at the baseline on each court with one on the deuce side and one on the ad side. Players on side A start at the net on each court with one on the deuce side and one on the ad side The instructor observes from behind the courts.
Description: Players start rallying down the line with the person facing them. Players on side B can only hit ground strokes. Players on side A can only hit volleys or overheads. Doubles alleys are in. The first team to reach 50 shots wins the drill.
Length: 5-8 min
Variation: More advanced players can only count volleys that are behind the service line.

4.

Name: Volley Warm-Up
Focus: Warm-up
Skill level: Intermediate, advanced
Setup: Players start at the net on each court with one on the deuce side and one on the ad side. The instructor observes from behind the courts.
Description: Players start volleying down the line with the person facing them. Doubles alleys are in. The first team to reach 50 shots wins the drill. Only volleys count.
Length: 5-8 min
Variation: Players have to volley from the service line.

5.

Name: Mini Tennis Warm-Up
Focus: Warm-up
Skill level: Intermediate, advanced
Setup: Players start at the service line on each court with one on the deuce side and one on the ad side. The instructor observes from behind the courts.
Description: The players play as a doubles team when each court. Each team can only hit the ball in the service boxes. Hard shots are not allowed. The first team to reach 15 points is the winner.
Length: 5-8 min
Variation: Hard shots are allowed for more advanced players.

6.

Name: Deep Shot Warm-Up (down the line)
Focus: Warm-up
Skill level: Advanced
Setup: Players start at the baseline on each court with one on the deuce side and one on the ad side. The instructor observes from behind the courts.
Description: Players start rallying down the line with the person facing them. Doubles alleys are in. Players only count the balls that go past the service line. The first team to reach 50 shots wins the drill.
Length: 5-10 min
Variation: Players are only allowed to hit their outside shots.

7.

Name: Deep Shot Warm-Up (crosscourt)
Focus: Warm-up
Skill level: Intermediate, advanced
Setup: Players start at the baseline on each court with one on the deuce side and one on the ad side. The instructor observes from behind the courts.
Description: Players start rallying crosscourt with the person across the court on the opposite side. Doubles alleys are in. Players only count the balls that go past the service line. The first team to reach 50 shots wins the drill. The players then switch positions from deuce side to ad side and repeat the drill.
Length: 5-10 min
Variation: Players are only allowed to hit their outside shots.

8.

Name: Alley Rally Warm-up (down the line)
Focus: Warm-up
Skill level: Intermediate, advanced
Setup: Players start at the baseline on each court with one on the deuce side and one on the ad side. The instructor observes from behind the courts.
Description: Players start rallying down the line with the person facing them. Players only count the balls that bounce in the doubles alleys. The first team to reach 50 shots wins the drill.
Length: 10-12 min
Variation: Players are only allowed to hit their outside shots.

Name: Alley Rally Warm-up (crosscourt)
Focus: Warm-up
Skill level: Intermediate, advanced
Setup: Players start at the baseline on each court with one on the deuce side and one on the ad side. The instructor observes from behind the courts.
Description: Players start rallying crosscourt with the person across the court on the opposite side. Players only count the balls that bounce in the doubles alleys. The first team to reach 50 shots wins the drill. The players then switch positions from deuce side to ad side and repeat the drill.
Length: 10-12 min
Variation: Players are only allowed to hit their outside shots.

10

Name: Alternating Shots Warm-up
Focus: Warm-up
Skill level: Intermediate, advanced
Setup: Two players start on each side at the baseline on each court in the middle. The instructor observes from behind the courts.
Description: The players start rallying on the singles court. Teammates alternate shots with each other within the point. The first court to reach 50 shots is the winner.
Length: 5-10 min
Variation: On each team, one player can only hit forehands and the other can only hit backhands. The players repeat the drill afterwards with their opposite shot.

II.   *Ground strokes*

Name: Half-Court Battle (down the line)
Focus: Ground strokes
Skill level: Intermediate, advanced
Setup: Players start at the baseline on each court with one on the deuce side and one on the ad side. The instructor observes from behind the courts.
Description: The courts are ranked from high to low. Players start rallying down the line with the person facing them. The points are played out half-court only. Volleys are allowed. Doubles alleys are in. Once a player reaches 15 points, everyone stops play. The players with more points are the winners. Winning players move up higher half a court; losing players move down half a court. The drill is repeated two or three more times.

Length: 10-15 min
Variation: Players can only hit their outside shots.

2.

Name: Half-Court Battle (crosscourt)
Focus: Ground strokes
Skill level: Intermediate, advanced
Setup: Players start at the baseline on each court with one on the deuce side and one on the ad side. The instructor observes from behind the courts.
Description: The courts are ranked from high to low. Players start rallying crosscourt with the person across the court on the opposite side. The points are played out half-court only. Volleys are allowed. Doubles alleys are in. Once a player reaches 15 points, everyone stops play. The players with more points are the winners. Winning players move up higher a full court; losing players move down a full court. The drill is repeated two or three more times.
Length: 10-15 min
Variation: Players can only hit their outside shots.

3.

Name: Deep Shot Battle
Focus: Ground strokes
Skill level: Advanced
Setup: Players start at the baseline on each court with one on the deuce side and one on the ad side. The instructor observes from behind the courts.
Description: The courts are ranked from high to low. Players start rallying down the line with the person facing them. The points are played out half-court only. Volleys are not allowed. Doubles alleys are in. The players can only hit the ball behind the service line. Once a player reaches 15 points, everyone stops play. The players with more points are the winners. Winning players move up higher half a court; losing players move down half a court. The drill is repeated two or three more times.
Length: 10-15 min
Variation: Players can only hit their outside shots.

4.

Name: Baseline Battle
Focus: Ground strokes
Skill level: Intermediate, advanced
Setup: Players form teams of two. Each team starts at the baseline on each court in the middle. The instructor observes from behind the courts.
Description: The courts are ranked from high to low. The first players on each team play

out the point on the singles court. The winning player stays in and the losing player switches with his partner. Players can not play more than three points in a row. Once a team reaches 15 points, everyone stops play. The teams with more points are the winners. Winning teams move up higher a full court; losing teams move down a full court. The drill is repeated two or three more times.
Length: 10-15 min
Variation: Winners can be worth two points.

5.

Name: Tricky Feed
Focus: Ground strokes
Skill level: Intermediate, advanced
Setup: Players form teams of two. Each team starts at the baseline on each court in the middle. The instructor observes from behind the courts.
Description: The courts are ranked from high to low. The first players on each team play out the point on the singles court. The player feeding the ball can hit any kind of feed. The only restriction is that he has to hit the feed underhand and from the baseline. The winning player stays in and the losing player switches with his partner. Teams alternate the feed. Players can not play more than three points in a row. Once a team reaches 15 points, everyone stops play. The teams with more points are the winners. Winning teams move up higher a full court; losing teams move down a full court. The drill is repeated two or three more times.
Length: 10-15 min
Variation: Winners can be worth two points.

6.

Name: Alternating Shots
Focus: Ground strokes
Skill level: Intermediate, advanced
Setup: Players form teams of two. Each team starts at the baseline on each court in the middle. The instructor observes from behind the courts.
Description: The courts are ranked from high to low. The teams play out the point against each other. Team members have to alternate shots within the point. Once a team reaches 15 points, everyone stops play. The teams with more points are the winners. Winning teams move up higher a full court; losing teams move down a full court. The drill is repeated two or three more times.
Length: 10-15 min
Variation: Winners can be worth two points.

7.

Name: 21 Point Drill
Focus: Ground strokes
Skill level: Intermediate, advanced
Setup: The drill is played on two courts. One player starts at each baseline on both courts. The rest of the players line up between the courts at the net post. The instructor observes from between the courts.
Description: The players on both courts play out the point against each other. The winning players stay in and the losing players go to the end of the line in the middle. The first player in line replaces the losing player. Players collect points individually. The first player to reach 21 points is the winner.
Length: 15-20 min
Variation: The instructor can feed the balls in from the middle.

8.

Name: Baseline Defender
Focus: Ground strokes
Skill level: Intermediate, advanced
Setup: The drill is played on two courts. The players form two teams. One player on each team starts at the baseline on side B. They are the defenders. The rest of the players line up behind the baseline on side A on different courts facing the defender from the other team. The instructor observes from behind the courts.
Description: The first player in each line feeds the ball in and plays out the point against the defender. The players go to the end of the line after each point, and the next player in line comes in. The points are played simultaneously on both courts. Once a team beats the defender seven times, the round ends and the team scores a point. A different player selected from each team to be the defender. The round is then repeated. The drill ends when every player has played as defender. The team with the most points wins the game.
Length: 15-20 min
Variation: The instructor can feed the ball in from between the courts.

9.

Name: The Ruler Drill
Focus: Ground strokes
Skill level: Intermediate, advanced
Setup: The drill is played on two courts. The sides on each court have a number. Side A on court 1 is #1, side B on court 1 is #2, side A one court 2 is #3, and side B on court 2 is #4. One player starts on #1 at the baseline, two players line up on #2 at the baseline, two players line up on #3 at the baseline, and the rest of the players line up on #4 at the baseline

also. The instructor observes from behind the courts.

Description: The player in the #1 position is the Ruler. The first players in line on both courts play out three points against each other. The players that win two out of the three points move up a position. The players that lose at #1 and #3 position move down a position. Players at #2 position only move down to #3 if a player moves up from #3. When a player moves up from the #3 position, the player who is waiting for his turn to play at #2 gets bumped down to #3. The player who is at the Ruler position after 10 minutes is the winner. Even though the drill sounds intimidating at first, it is very popular and players catch on fast once they start playing.

Length: 10 min

Variation: Players can play five points to determine the winner.

10.

Name: Deep Shot Baseline Battle

Focus: Ground strokes

Skill level: Advanced

Setup: Players form teams of two. Each team starts at the baseline on each court in the middle. The instructor observes from behind the courts.

Description: The courts are ranked from high to low. The first players on each team play out the point. Players can only hit the ball behind the service line. The winning player stays in and the losing player switches with his partner. Players can not play more than three points in a row. Once a team reaches 15 points, everyone stops play. The teams with more points are the winners. Winning teams move up higher a full court; losing teams move down a full court. The drill is repeated two or three more times.

Length: 10-15 min

Variation: Hitting a winner can be worth two points.

III. *Net approach*

1.

Name: Half-Court Approach

Focus: Net approach

Skill level: Intermediate, advanced

Setup: Players start at the baseline on each court with one on the deuce side and one on the ad side. The instructor observes from behind the courts.

Description: The courts are ranked from high to low. Players feed short balls and play out the point down the line with the person facing them. The points are played out half-court only. Players alternate the feed. Doubles alleys are in. Once a player reaches 15 points, everyone stops play. The players with more points are the winners. Winning players move up higher half a court; losing players move down half a court. The drill is repeated two or three more times.

Length: 10-12 min

Variation: Winning the point with a volley is worth two points.

2.

Name: Full Court Approach

Focus: Net approach

Skill level: Intermediate, advanced

Setup: Players form teams of two. Each team starts at the baseline on each court in the middle. The instructor observes from behind the courts.

Description: The courts are ranked from high to low. The first players on each team play out the point. Players feed a short ball in each point. The winning player stays in and the losing player switches with his partner. Teams alternate the feed. No player can play more than three points in a row. Once a team reaches 15 points, everyone stops play. The teams with more points are the winners. Winning teams move up higher a full court; losing teams move down a full court. The drill is repeated two or three more times.

Length: 10-15 min

Variation: Winning the point with a volley is worth two points.

3.

Name: Doubles Approach

Focus: Net approach

Skill level: Intermediate, advanced

Setup: Players form teams of two. Each team starts at the baseline on each court with one player on the deuce and one player on the ad side. The instructor observes from behind the courts.

Description: The courts are ranked from high to low. Teams play the points out as doubles teams. Players feed a short ball crosscourt in each point. Teams alternate the feed. Once a team reaches 15 points, everyone stops play. The teams with more points are the winners. Winning teams move up higher a full court; losing teams move down a full court. The drill is repeated two or three more times.

Length: 10-15 min

Variation: Winning the point with a volley is worth two points.

4.

Name: Approach Defenders

Focus: Net approach

Skill level: Intermediate, advanced

Setup: The drill is played on two courts. One random player starts on side A on both courts. They are the defenders. The rest of the players form a single line behind the baseline on side B on both courts. The instructor feeds the ball from between the courts from side A.

Description: The instructor feeds a short ball to court 1 and a short ball to court 2 simultaneously. The first players in each line approach the net and play out a point against the defenders. The attackers go to the end of the opposite line after the point. Once a player beats the defenders three times, he switches with a defender he just beat. The defenders score a point every time they win a rally. The game ends when a defender has 15 points.

Length: 10-15 min

Variation: An attacker can become defender only if he beats both defenders in a row. If he beats one defender but loses to the other, he has to start over.

5.

Name: Approach Battle

Focus: Net approach

Skill level: Intermediate, advanced

Setup: Players form teams of two. Each team starts at the baseline on each court in the middle. The instructor observes from behind the courts.

Description: The courts are ranked from high to low. The first players on each team play out the point. Winning the point with a volley is worth two points. The winning player stays in and the losing player switches with his partner. Teams alternate the feed. No player can play more than three points in a row. Once a team reaches 15 points, everyone stops play. The teams with more points are the winners. Winning teams move up higher a full court; losing teams move down a full court. The drill is repeated two or three more times.

Length: 10-15 min

Variation: Hitting a volley that is also a winner is worth three points.

6.

Name: Second Serve Attack

Focus: Net approach

Skill level: Intermediate, advanced

Setup: Players form teams of two. Each team starts at the baseline on each court in the middle. The instructor observes from behind the courts.

Description: The courts are ranked from high to low. The first players in each team play out the point with only one serve. The receiving player can score 2 points by winning the point with a volley. The winning player stays in and the losing player switches with his partner. Teams alternate serves. No player can play more than three points in a row. Once a team reaches 15 points, everyone stops play. The teams with more points are the winners. Winning teams move up higher a full court; losing teams move down a full court. The drill is repeated two or three more times.

Length: 10-15 min
Variation: The receiving team can also score 2 points by winning the point with the return.

7.

Name: Serve and Volley Drill
Focus: Net approach
Skill level: Intermediate, advanced
Setup: Players form teams of two. Each team starts at the baseline on each court in the middle. The instructor observes from behind the courts.
Description: The courts are ranked from high to low. The first players in each team play out the point with serve. The server has to serve and volley both the first and second serves and has a chance to score 2 points with a volley. The winning player stays in and the losing player switches with his partner. Teams alternate serves. No player can play more than three points in a row. Once a team reaches 15 points, everyone stops play. The teams with more points are the winners. Winning teams move up higher a full court; losing teams move down a full court. The drill is repeated two or three more times.
Length: 10-15 min
Variation: Hitting a winning volley on the second serve point is worth three points.

8.

Name: Short Ball Battle
Focus: Net approach
Skill level: Intermediate, advanced
Setup: Players form teams of two. Each team starts at the baseline on each court in the middle. The instructor observes from behind the courts.
Description: The courts are ranked from high to low. The first players on each team play out the point. Players on not allowed to hit volleys until they receive a short ball. The player yells out "short", and from that point volleys are allowed. Winning the point with a volley is worth two points. The winning player stays in and the losing player switches with his partner. Teams alternate the feed. No player can play more than three points in a row. Once a team reaches 15 points, everyone stops play. The teams with more points are the winners. Winning teams move up higher a full court; losing teams move down a full court. The drill is repeated two or three more times.
Length: 10-15 min
Variation: Only the player who yelled out "short" can score 2 points with a volley.

9.

Name: One Bounce Doubles
Focus: Net approach

Skill level: Intermediate, advanced

Setup: Players form teams of two. Each team starts at the baseline on each court with one player on the deuce and one player on the ad side. The instructor observes from behind the courts.

Description: The courts are ranked from high to low. Teams play the points out as doubles teams. The ball can only bounce one time on each side during each point. Teams alternate the feed. Once a team reaches 15 points, everyone stops play. The teams with more points are the winners. Winning teams move up higher a full court; losing teams move down a full court. The drill is repeated two or three more times.

Length: 8-10 min

Variation: Hitting winners is worth two points.

10.

Name: 21 Point Drill with Short Balls

Focus: Net approach

Skill level: Intermediate, advanced

Setup: The drill is played on two courts. One player starts at each baseline on both courts. The rest of the players line up between the courts at the net post. The instructor observes from between the courts.

Description: A random player on both courts feeds a short ball and plays out the point against the player on the opposite side. The winning players stay in and the losing players go to the end of the line in the middle. The first player in line replaces the losing player. The winning players always feed the short balls. Players collect points individually. The first player to reach 21 points is the winner.

Length: 10-15 min

Variation: The instructor can feed the short balls from the net post.

IV.   _Net play_

1.

Name: Half-Court Volleys

Focus: Net play

Skill level: Intermediate, advanced

Setup: Players on side A start at the baseline on each court with one on the deuce side and one on the ad side. Players on side B start at the net on each court with one on the deuce side and one on the ad side. The instructor observes from behind the courts.

Description: The courts are ranked from high to low. The players at the baseline feed the ball in and play to point out against the net player facing them. The points are played out half-court only. Doubles alleys are in. Once a player reaches 8 points, players switch positions. When any player reaches 15 points, everyone stops play. The players with more points are the winners. Winning players move up higher half a court; losing players move down half a court. The drill is repeated two or three more times.

Length: 8-10 min

Variation: Hitting a winner is worth two points.

2.

Name: Half-Court Overheads

Focus: Net play

Skill level: Intermediate, advanced

Setup: Players on side B start at the baseline on each court with one on the deuce side and one on the ad side. Players on side A start at the net on each court with one on the deuce side and one on the ad side. The instructor observes from behind the courts.

Description: The courts are ranked from high to low. The players at the net feed the ball in and play to point out against the baseline player facing them. The points are played out half-court only. Doubles alleys are in. The net players are not allowed to step behind the service line. The baseline players are encouraged to hit lobs. Once a player reaches 8 points, players switch positions. When any player reaches 15 points, everyone stops play. The players with more points are the winners. Winning players move up higher half a court; losing players move down half a court. The drill is repeated two or three more times.

Length: 8-10 min

Variation: The baseline players feed a lob to start the point. The net players can step behind the service line.

3.

Name: Half-Court Volley to Volley

Focus: Net play

Skill level: Intermediate, advanced

Setup: Players start at the net on each court with one on the deuce side and one on the ad side. The instructor observes from behind the courts.

Description: The courts are ranked from high to low. Players start volleying down the line with the person facing them. The points are played out half-court only. Doubles alleys are in. Once a player reaches 15 points, everyone stops play. The players with more points are the winners. Winning players move up higher half a court; losing players move down half a court. The drill is repeated two or three more times.

Length: 8-10 min

Variation: Hitting a winner is worth two points.

Name: Net Defender
Focus: Net play
Skill level: Intermediate, advanced
Setup: The drill is played on two courts. The players form two teams. One player on each team starts at the net on side A. They are the defenders. The rest of the players line up behind the baseline on side B on different courts facing the defender from the other team. The instructor feeds from side A.
Description: The instructor feeds the ball to the first players in line on both courts who play out the point against the defender. The players go to the end of the line after each point, and the next player in line comes in. The points are played simultaneously on both courts. Once a team beats the defender seven times, the round ends and the team scores a point. A different player selected from each team to be the defender. The round is then repeated. The drill ends when every player has played as defender. The team with the most points wins the game.
Length: 15-20 min
Variation: The net players can feed the ball instead of the instructor.

5

Name: Ruler of 2 Courts (singles)
Focus: Net play
Skill level: Intermediate, advanced
Setup: The drill is played on two courts. Two random players start at the net on side A with one on each court. They are the rulers. The rest of the players form a single line at the baseline on side B on both courts. They are the challengers. The instructor feeds from side A.
Description: The instructor feeds a ball to both courts to the first players in line who play out the points against the rulers. The challengers switch courts after each point. The challengers try to win three points against the rulers to take their spot. If a challenger wins the third point against a ruler, he switches with that player. Only rulers keep their score, and the game ends when one of them reaches 15 points.
Length: 10-15 min
Variation: The challengers have to beat each ruler one time. If a challenger wins the first point but loses the second, he starts over from zero.

Name: Ruler of 2 Courts (doubles)
Focus: Net play
Skill level: Intermediate, advanced
Setup: The drill is played on two courts. The players form two player teams. Two random

teams start at the net on side A with one on each court. They are the rulers. The rest of the teams line up behind each other at the baseline on side B on both courts. They are the challengers. The instructor feeds from side A.

Description: The instructor feeds a ball to both courts to the first teams in line who play out the points against the rulers. The challengers switch courts after each point. The challengers try to win three points against the rulers to take their spot. If a challenger team wins the third point against a ruler team, he switches with that team. Only rulers keep their score, and the game ends when one of them reaches 15 points.

Length: 10-15 min

Variation: The challengers have to beat each ruler one time. If a challenger wins the first point but loses the second, he starts over from zero.

7.

Name: Volley 21 Point Drill (singles)

Focus: Net play

Skill level: Intermediate, advanced

Setup: The drill is played on two courts. One player starts at each baseline on side B both courts. One player starts at each net position on side A both courts. The rest of the players line up between the courts at the net post. The instructor observes from between the courts.

Description: The net players feed the ball in and the players on both courts play out the point against each other. The winning players stay in and play the next point from the baseline. The losing players go to the end of the line in the middle. The first player in line replaces the losing player and plays the next point from the net. The player coming in is always the net player. Net players always feed the ball. Players collect points individually. The first player to reach 21 points is the winner.

Length: 10-15 min

Variation: The instructor can feed the ball each point from between the courts to the baseline players.

8.

Name: Volley 21 Point Drill (doubles)

Focus: Net play

Skill level: Intermediate, advanced

Setup: The drill is played on two courts. Players form teams of two. One team starts at each baseline on side B both courts. One team starts at each net position on side A both courts. The rest of the teams line up between the courts at the net post. The instructor observes from between the courts.

Description: The net teams feed the ball in and the teams on both courts play out the point against each other. The winning teams stay in and play the next point from the baseline. The losing teams go to the end of the line in the middle. The first team in line replaces the losing team and plays the next point from the net. The team coming always starts at the net. Net teams always feed the ball. Doubles teams collect points individually. The first team to reach 21 points is the winner.

Length: 10-15 min

Variation: The instructor can feed the ball each point from between the courts to the baseline teams.

9.

Name: One Point Singles Tournament (volleys)

Focus: Net play

Skill level: Intermediate, advanced

Setup: The drill is played on two courts. There are four positions in this drill: the service lines on side A on both courts, and the service lines on side B on both courts. One player starts at each position. If there are leftover players, they start behind any player at any position. The instructor feeds from side A.

Description: The instructor feeds to both players on side B who play out the point against the players facing them. The losing player is out of the game. The winning player moves clockwise to the end of the line at the next position. Once there are only three players, they switch to only one court. The final two players don't have to switch at the end. The surviving player is the winner.

Length: 5-10 min

Variation: Players can start with more than one life to make the game longer.

10.

Name: One Point Doubles Tournament (volleys)

Focus: Net play

Skill level: Intermediate, advanced

Setup: The drill is played on two courts. The players form teams of two. There are four positions in this drill: the service lines on side A on both courts, and the service lines on side B on both courts. One team starts at each position. If there are leftover teams, they start behind any team at any position. The instructor feeds from side A.

Description: The instructor feeds to both teams on side B who play out the point against the teams facing them. The losing team is out of the game. The winning team moves clockwise to the end of the line at the next position. Once there are only three teams, they switch to only one court. The final two teams don't have to switch at the end. The surviving team is the winner.

Length: 5-10 min

Variation: Teams can start with more than one life to make the game longer.

V.   *Serve and return*

1.

Name: 21 Point Drill with serve
Focus: Serve and return
Skill level: Intermediate, advanced
Setup: The drill is played on two courts. One player starts at each baseline on both courts. The rest of the players line up between the courts at the net post. The instructor observes from between the courts.
Description: The players on both courts serve and play out the point against each other. The players serve to the deuce side on one court and to the ad side on the other court. The winning players stay in and the losing players go to the end of the line in the middle. The first player in line replaces the losing player and becomes the server for the next point. Players collect points individually. The first player to reach 21 points is the winner.
Length: 10-15 min
Variation: Hitting a winner can be worth two points.

2.

Name: One Point Singles Tournament
Focus: Serve and return
Skill level: Intermediate, advanced
Setup: The drill is played on two courts. There are four positions in this drill: the baselines on side A on both courts, and the baselines on side B on both courts. One player starts at each position. If there are leftover players, they start behind any player at any position. The instructor observes from between the courts.
Description: The players on side A are the servers, and the players on side B are the receivers. The losing player is out of the game. The winning player moves clockwise to the end of the line at the next position. Once there are only three players, they switch to only one court. The final two players don't have to switch at the end. The surviving player is the winner.
Length: 5-10 min
Variation: Players can start with more than one life to make the game longer.

3.

Name: Half-Court Point Play (crosscourt)
Focus: Serve and return
Skill level: Intermediate, advanced
Setup: Players start at the baseline on each court with one on the deuce side and one on

the ad side. The instructor observes from behind the courts.

Description: The courts are ranked from high to low. Players on side A start the point with a serve and play out the point crosscourt with the person across the court on the opposite side. The points are played out half-court only. Volleys are allowed. Doubles alleys are in. A different player serves after each two points. Once a player reaches 15 points, everyone stops play. The players with more points are the winners. Winning players move up higher a full court; losing players move down a full court. The drill is repeated two or three more times.

Length: 10-15 min

Variation: Winning the point with a volley is worth two points.

4.

Name: Baseline Battle with Serves

Focus: Serve and return

Skill level: Intermediate, advanced

Setup: Players form teams of two. Each team starts at the baseline on each court in the middle. The instructor observes from behind the courts.

Description: The courts are ranked from high to low. The first players on each team play out the point against each other on the singles court. A random player starts the first point with a serve. Afterwards, the winning player serves the next point. Points are alternated between the deuce and the ad sides. The winning player stays in and the losing player switches with his partner. Players can not play more than three points in a row. Once a team reaches 15 points, everyone stops play. The teams with more points are the winners. Winning teams move up higher a full court; losing teams move down a full court. The drill is repeated two or three more times.

Length: 10-15 min

Variation: Winners can be worth two points.

5.

Name: Return Defender (singles)

Focus: Serve and return

Skill level: Intermediate, advanced

Setup: The drill is played on two courts. The players form two teams. One player on each team starts in return position on the deuce side on side B. They are the defenders. The rest of the players line up behind the baseline on side A on different courts facing the defender from the other team. The instructor observes from behind the courts.

Description: The first player in each line serves the ball and plays out the point against the defender. The players go to the end of the line after each point, and the next player in line comes in. The points are played simultaneously on both courts. The points are alternated between the deuce and the ad sides on each court. Once a team beats the defender seven times, the round ends and the team scores a point. A different player selected from each team to be the defender. The round is then repeated. The drill ends when every player has played as defender. The team with the most points wins the game.

Length: 15-20 min

Variation: Hitting a winner on the defender scores two points.

6.

Name: Return Defender (doubles)

Focus: Serve and return

Skill level: Intermediate, advanced

Setup: The drill is played on two courts. The players form two teams. Two players on each team starts in one up, one back position on the deuce side on side B. They are the defenders. The rest of the players line up behind the baseline on side A on different courts facing the defenders from the other team. The first two players from this line start in one up one back formation on side A. The instructor observes from behind the courts.

Description: The first two players in each line serve the ball and play out the point against the defenders. The players go to the end of the line after each point, and the next two players in line come in. The points are played simultaneously on both courts. The points are alternated between the deuce and the ad sides on each court. Once a team beats the defender seven times, the round ends and the team scores a point. Different two players are selected from each team to be defenders. The round is then repeated. The drill ends when every player has played as defender at least once. The team with the most points wins the game.

Length: 15-20 min

Variation: Hitting a winner on the defenders scores two points.

7.

Name: Return Baseline Battle

Focus: Serve and return

Skill level: Intermediate, advanced

Setup: Players form teams of two. Each team starts at the baseline on each court in the middle. The instructor observes from behind the courts.

Description: The courts are ranked from high to low. The first players on each team play out the point against each other on the singles court starting with a serve. The return has to go crosscourt. A random player serves the first point, but the winning player serves the next point afterwards. Points are alternated between the deuce and the ad sides. The winning player stays in and the losing player switches with his partner. Players can not play more than three points in a row. Once a team reaches 15 points, everyone stops play. The teams with more points are the winners. Winning teams move up higher a full court; losing teams move down a full court. The drill is repeated two or three more times.

Length: 10-15 min
Variation: The returns have to go down the line.

8.

Name: Baseline Battle Doubles
Focus: Serve and return
Skill level: Intermediate, advanced
Setup: This drill is played on two courts. About equal amount of players start on each half on both courts. Two random players on each team start in one up one back formation on the deuce side. The rest of the players start behind their teammates. The instructor observes from the net post.
Description: A random player starts the first point with a serve. Afterwards, the winning team serves the next point. Points are played only on the deuce. The winning players stay in and the losing players rotate positions in a counterclockwise order. The same team can not play more than three points in a row. Once a team reaches 10 points, teams switch to the ad side. The team that first reaches 20 points is the winner.
Length: 10-15 min
Variation: Hitting a winner is worth two points.

9.

Name: Rulers of the Court with Serve
Focus: Server and return
Skill level: Intermediate, advanced
Setup: This drill is played on two courts. The players form teams of two. A random team starts on side B in one up one back formation on the deuce side on court 1. Another random team starts on side B in one up one back formation on the ad side on court 2. These two teams are the rulers. The rest of the teams start on side A divided equally on the two courts. They are the challengers. The instructor observes from the net post.
Description: Points are always played on the deuce side on court 1 and always on the ad side on court 2. The first challenger team on each court comes forward and plays out the point against the rulers with a serve. Challengers always serve every point. After each point, the challengers go to the end of the line on the other court. Once they beat each ruler one time in a row, they become rulers. They switch with the ruler team they beat the second time. Only the rulers keep score. Once a team has 10 points, the drill ends and the team wins.
Length: 15-10 min
Variation: Challenger teams stay in if they win the first point. They have to beat the rulers from both the deuce and the ad side to take their spot. They still have to go to the end of the line on the other court if they lose the point.

Name: Serve and Return Rotation
Focus: Serve and return
Skill level: Intermediate, advanced
Setup: Players start at the baseline on each court with one on the deuce side and one on the ad side. The players on side B are the receivers, and the players on side A are the servers. The instructor observes from behind the courts.
Description: Each server has two chances the serve. The receivers have to return the ball crosscourt. Doubles alleys are in. The point is not played out afterwards. The servers rotate positions clockwise. The receivers keep their positions. The receivers score points every time they hit a successful return crosscourt. Only the receivers score points in this drill. Once a server hits three serves that are not returned, he becomes a receiver. He switches with the receiver he beat on the third serve. Once a player reaches 15 points, the game ends and the player is the winner.
Length: 10-15 min
Variation: Lower level players only have to hit two unreturnable serves to become receivers.

Definitions

1 up 1 back position – the most common doubles position where one player starts at the baseline and the other player starts at the net

1 up 1 back position on the deuce side – the baseline player is on the deuce side and the net player is on the ad side

1 up 1 back position on the ad side – the baseline player is on the ad side and the net players on the deuce side

2 back position – a doubles position where both players start at the baseline

Ad side – facing the net it is the left half of the court

Advanced level – includes NTRP rating 4.0 or higher, college players, professional players, nationally ranked juniors

Alley – refers to the doubles alleys on both sides of the court

Approach shot – a transitional shot hit between the baseline in the net position, allows the player to attack the net

Attacking – approaching the net or controlling the point from the baseline

Attacking the net – approaching the net

Baseline – the line that runs from the left to the right of the court at the very back

Beginner level – includes NTRP rating 2.5 or lower, players just starting out playing tennis, age 8 or younger

Clinic – instructional class with more than four players

Crosscourt – hitting from deuce side to deuce side or ad side to ad side

Deuce side – facing the net it is the right half of the court

Doubles alley – the area between the doubles sideline and the single sidelines on both sides of the court

Doubles side line – the lines on the very left and right sides of the court

Down the line – hitting from deuce side to ad side or ad side to deuce side

Drop shot – hitting the shortest ball possible just behind the net usually with some backspin

Footwork – refers to endurance, court positioning, shot setup, speed, and efficient movement

Half volley – blocking the ball back immediately after it bounced

Instructor – refers to tennis instructors, coaches, tennis teachers, and tennis professionals

Intermediate level – includes NTRP rating 3.0 to 3.5, most high school players, between age 8 and 14

Lob – hitting a high ball over a player at the net or getting high deep balls

Middle service line – the line separating the two service boxes

Net approach – players transitioning from the baseline position to net position during a rally

Net play – includes any shot hit in the net position, usually refers to volleys and overheads

Net post – one of the two columns that hold up the net

Overhead – striking a ball with a full swing at the highest possible point usually at the net position

Passing shot – hitting the ball past the net player or players with a ground stroke

Player – refers to the people participating in the drill

Poaching – a tactic in doubles where the net players try to intercept baseline rallies by crossing over to the partner's side

Private lesson – a one on one instructional lesson with the tennis instructor

Return position – a starting position for players returning a serve behind one of the service boxes, usually around the baseline

Semi-private lesson – an instructional lesson for two players with the tennis instructor

Service box – the two rectangles behind the net on both sides of the court

Service line – the line that runs along at the end of the two service boxes on both sides

Serving position – a position behind the baseline on the deuce or the ad side where players start the point with a serve

Side A – close side

Side B – far side

Singles side line – the second sidelines from the outside of the court after the doubles sidelines

Slice – any shot hit with backspin

Smash – synonymous with overhead

Swinging volley – a volley hit from any point of the court with a full swing

T – the point where the middle service line meets the service line

Topspin – any shot hit with forward spin

Volley – any shot that is hit in the air without a bounce

Winner – any shot that bounces twice on the opponent's side

Winning shot – the last good shot of the point

Drill Sheet

Name:

Focus:

Skill level:

Setup:

Description:

Length:

Variation:

Notes

47191755R00093

Made in the USA
San Bernardino, CA
11 August 2019